THE UPPER ROOM®

WHERE THE WORLD MEETS TO PRAY

Susan Hibbins
UK Editor

INTERDENOMINATIONAL
INTERNATIONAL
INTERRACIAL

33 LANGUAGES
Multiple formats are available in some languages

The Bible Reading Fellowship
15 The Chambers, Vineyard
Abingdon OX14 3FE
brf.org.uk

The Bible Reading Fellowship (BRF) is a Registered Charity (233280)

ISBN 978 0 85746 606 8
All rights reserved

Originally published in the USA by The Upper Room®
US edition © The Upper Room®
This edition © The Bible Reading Fellowship 2018
Cover image by Rebecca J Hall

Acknowledgements

Scripture quotations marked NRSV are taken from The New Revised Standard Version of the Bible, Anglicised Edition, copyright © 1989, 1995 by the Division of Christian Education of the National Council of the Churches of Christ in the USA. Used by permission. All rights reserved.

Scripture quotations marked NIV are taken from The Holy Bible, New International Version (Anglicised edition) copyright © 1979, 1984, 2011 by Biblica. Used by permission of Hodder & Stoughton Publishers, an Hachette UK company. All rights reserved. 'NIV' is a registered trademark of Biblica. UK trademark number 1448790.

Extracts marked KJV are from the Authorized Version of the Bible (The King James Bible), the rights in which are vested in the Crown, reproduced by permission of the Crown's Patentee, Cambridge University Press.

Extracts from CEB are copyright © 2011 by Common English Bible.

Printed by Gutenberg Press, Tarxien, Malta

The Upper Room is ideal in helping us spend a quiet time with God each day. Each daily entry is based on a passage of scripture, and is followed by a meditation and prayer. Each person who contributes a meditation to the magazine seeks to relate their experience of God in a way that will help those who use *The Upper Room* every day.

Here are some guidelines to help you make best use of *The Upper Room*:

1   Read the passage of Scripture. It is a good idea to read it more than once, in order to have a fuller understanding of what it is about and what you can learn from it.
2   Read the meditation. How does it relate to your own experience? Can you identify with what the writer has outlined from their own experience or understanding?
3   Pray the written prayer. Think about how you can use it to relate to people you know, or situations that need your prayers today.
4   Think about the contributor who has written the meditation. Some *Upper Room* users include this person in their prayers for the day.
5   Meditate on the 'Thought for the day' and the 'Prayer focus', perhaps using them again as the focus for prayer or direction for action.

Why is it important to have a daily quiet time? Many people will agree that it is the best way of keeping in touch every day with the God who sustains us, and who sends us out to do his will and show his love to the people we encounter each day. Meeting with God in this way reassures us of his presence with us, helps us to discern his will for us and makes us part of his worldwide family of Christian people through our prayers.

I hope that you will be encouraged as you use the magazine regularly as part of your daily devotions, and that God will richly bless you as you read his word and seek to learn more about him.

Susan Hibbins
UK Editor

In times of/For help with . . .

Below is a list of entries in this copy of *The Upper Room* relating to situations or emotions with which we may need help:

Anger: Jul 27; Aug 8

Assurance: May 22; Jun 14, 29; Jul 11, 31; Aug 10, 27

Bible reading: May 9, 10, 19; Jun 2; Jul 29; Aug 1, 6, 13, 16

Change: Jul 3, 8

Christian community: May 6, 29; Jun 3, 6, 19; Jul 4, 28, 30; Aug 9, 15

Compassion: May 16; Aug 22, 29

Creation: May 11; Jun 24; Jul 2, 23; Aug 24

Doubt: May 31; Jun 15, 26; Jul 5, 16

Encouragement: May 5, 10, 24, 28; Jun 6, 8; Jul 9, 16, 31

Family: May 9, 13, 20; Jun 2, 17, 29; Aug 5, 13

Fear: May 4, 12, 23, 25; Jun 14; Jul 3, 18, 24, 27

Forgiveness: May 23; Jul 21

Friendship: May 23; Jul 9, 28; Aug 28

Giving: May 17; Jun 7, 10; Jul 4; Aug 14

Grief: May 21; Jun 12, 21, 29; Jul 7; Aug 28

God's goodness/love: May 5, 18, 22; Jun 11, 12; Jul 2, 10, 31; Aug 19, 20, 28

God's presence: May 4, 24, 25; Jun 3, 9, 21; Jul 5, 7, 16; Aug 10, 30, 31

God's provision: May 1, 11; Jun 6, 20; Jul 11, 18, 25; Aug 3, 11

Gratitude: May 8, 30; Jun 20; Jul 2, 11, 23; Aug 2, 18

Growth: May 3, 14, 18, 26; Jun 5; Jul 1; Aug 1, 15

Guidance: May 18, 21; Jun 5, 30; Jul 3, 8, 22; Aug 7, 9

Healing/illness: May 8, 13, 16, 20, 24; Jun 14; Jul 12, 19; Aug 8, 20, 30

Hope: May 20; Jun 18; Jul 12; Aug 5, 24

Hospitality: May 29; Aug 26

Job issues: May 6, 24; Jun 10, 16, 30; Jul 25; Aug 3, 21

Judging: May 26; Jun 23; Jul 26; Aug 14, 22, 26

Living our faith: May 3, 9, 31; Jun 15, 22, 24; Jul 1, 10, 19; Aug 7, 25, 29

Loss: May 16; Jul 28; Aug 4

Mental illness: May 13

Mission/outreach: Jun 22, 27, 28; Jul 20, 24

New beginnings: May 11, 15, 23; Jun 16, 22, 28

Obedience: May 27; Jun 11, 16, 30; Jul 6, 20; Aug 25

Parenting: May 9, 18, 22; Jun 11, 17; Jul 31

Patience: May 10, 20, 27; Jun 18, 30; Aug 9, 18

Peace/unrest: May 4, 7; Jun 8; Jul 27; Aug 10, 31

Prayer: May 7, 13, 30; Jun 13, 19, 25; Jul 8, 15, 30; Aug 8, 15, 31

Renewal: May 8, 11, 16; Jul 14

Repentance: May 23, 26; Jun 23; Jul 13

Salvation: Aug 16

Serving: May 17, 29; Jun 4, 7, 27; Aug 17, 22

Sin: May 14; Jul 13

Speaking about faith: Jun 22; Jul 15, 21; Aug 17

Spiritual gifts: Jun 22; Jul 17; Aug 14, 26, 29

Spiritual practices: May 3, 27, 30; Jun 2, 5; Jul 6, 14, 23; Aug 1, 2, 23

Tragedy: Aug 28

Trust: May 1, 12; Jun 3, 7, 15, 26

Weakness: Jun 14; Jul 22, 24; Aug 3, 5, 21

Worry: May 6, 7; Jun 3, 9; Jul 14, 29; Aug 4, 18, 23

Jesus said, 'Remember, I am with you always, to the end of the age.'
Matthew 28:20 (NRSV)

After the Day of Pentecost, Christians who follow a liturgical calendar enter the season known as 'Ordinary Time', which lasts until Advent and occupies a significant portion of the Christian calendar. The name seems fitting since no major Christian festivals occur during this season.

When I was young, I thought Ordinary Time sounded boring. We weren't actively anticipating Christ's birth at Christmas or focusing on the disciplines of Lent. Ordinary Time felt long, uneventful and thoroughly unexciting.

Now that I am an adult, Ordinary Time holds for me the comfort of familiarity. It also holds particular promise: God is with us – not just for big events or important celebrations but in the unremarkable moments of each day.

Some of the meditations in this issue describe the comfort and peace, as well as the challenges, that come with a deep sense of God's presence in daily life. The idea that God is with us is a thread that runs throughout scripture, and it appears often when I read devotional writing. That God is with us during the extraordinary moments of our lives as well as the mundane and uneventful ones is a message that feels particularly appropriate for the long, unremarkable season of Ordinary Time. The assurance that God is with us today and always is worth hearing again and again, and it may make this season not quite so unremarkable after all.

Lindsay L. Gray
Editorial Director, The Upper Room

Editions of *The Upper Room* daily devotional guide are printed in:

- Australia
- Indonesia
- Malaysia
- Myanmar
- The Philippines
- Singapore
- Thailand

Indonesia
Every month, the publishing team of *Saat Teduh*, the Indonesian edition of *The Upper Room*, visits a local prison. They lead a service for the inmates, pray with them, and share copies of the devotional.

Thailand
The publisher of the Thai edition of *The Upper Room*, The Church of Christ in Thailand, broadcasts each day's meditation on the radio, reaching people in rural areas of the country.

The Editor writes...

Recently I was reading the story in John's Gospel in which Jesus spent time talking with a Samaritan woman who had come to get water from the well where Jesus was resting (John 4:1–26). The conversation includes some of Jesus' most well-known words: 'Whoever drinks the water I give them will never thirst. Indeed, the water I give them will become in them a spring of water welling up to eternal life' (v. 14, NIV). After talking with Jesus, the woman is so inspired by what he has told her that she abandons her water jar to run back to the town and tell all her neighbours about him; many of them later believed in him after listening to Jesus themselves.

I wonder what the woman thought about this milestone in her life in later years, perhaps as she became older and more reflective. Did she close her eyes and remember that far-off day, the sunshine and the heat, the heavy water jar that she gratefully set down to talk to the young man who sat by the well? Did she recall Jesus' words about living water, not realising at the time that it was the most precious conversation she would ever have? Perhaps she remembered his kindness, his smile, his willingness to talk to her, a woman whom many regarded as having dubious morals. She didn't know who Jesus was when she talked to him that day, but did she try to get news of him and his teaching after he left? How did she live her life with Jesus' words in her heart?

What is our own reaction to Jesus' words? Do they change our lives? Sometimes when we read the Bible, especially familiar passages, we might feel that they have nothing new to add to our understanding. Yet there are times when the words seem to leap off the page and speak directly to our situation, providing comfort, challenge or direction. In our own time, Jesus' living water is available to us as surely as it was for one individual one hot day by a well.

Susan Hibbins
UK Editor

The Bible readings are selected with great care, and we urge you to include the suggested reading in your devotional time.

Eating rocks?

Read Psalm 37:1–9

Let him lead me to the banquet hall, and let his banner over me be love.
Song of Songs 2:4 (NIV)

I found my toddler on the stairs, contentedly shoving pebbles into his mouth. I fished the pebbles out and carried him to the table to eat dessert. He didn't appreciate that. He flailed and screamed, frustrated that I would tear him away from his treasure. But when he finally saw the chocolate cake at the table, he stopped screaming and his eyes widened with joy.

The adults at the table laughed, because who would willingly choose pebbles over chocolate cake? But don't I do the same every day? I contentedly fill my life with meaningless activities and things. I grin, happy with what I've gained. I'm just like my son: sitting on the stairs, thinking I have found pure joy. But really God wants to invite me to the banquet table where I can find true joy. I am frustrated when what I want is taken away, not realising what glory is waiting just beyond my sight. I want to delight in the Lord and replace my own desires with desires that lead to God. I want him to teach me to love and seek true joy.

Prayer: *Dear God, help us to trust in your love. Direct our thoughts and desires toward you and the true joy you offer. Amen*

Thought for the day: Today I will let God lead me to the banquet table.

Christie Thomas (Alberta, Canada)

PRAYER FOCUS: FOR GOD'S DESIRES TO BE MY DESIRES

Rooted in Christ

Read Ephesians 3:14–19

So then, just as you received Christ Jesus as Lord, continue to live your lives in him, rooted and strengthened in the faith as you were taught, and overflowing with thankfulness.
Colossians 2:6–7 (NIV)

On a sunny day I visited a beautiful Scottish botanic garden, famous for its hilly woodland trail. My husband drew my attention to an ancient Scots pine tree. It rose out of the ground at an acute angle and looked as if it would fall at any moment onto a footpath. The weight of the long, thick trunk must have been enormous. But the manager of the estate said it was safe. The strength and amazing capability of the root system was saving it from collapse, though the power was unseen to the onlooker. The tree survived because its roots sank deep to provide a stable and strong foundation, bringing life-giving water to every part of the tree.

We who belong to the Lord Jesus are rooted firmly in him, an anchor for our faith. He is our foundation, and through the Holy Spirit we drink his water of life springing up within us.

On our journey of faith there are times when we are buffeted by the storms of life and we can be tested to breaking point. But like the tree we don't collapse, because Christ is holding us, lovingly working out his purposes for our good and his glory.

Prayer: *Dear Lord Jesus, help us to become rooted in you, knowing that you will never let us fall. Amen*

Thought for the day: We are grounded and safe in Jesus' love.

Janette Hughson (West Lothian, Scotland)

Your way over ours

Read Matthew 6:16–18

When you fast, put oil on your head and wash your face.
Matthew 6:17 (NIV)

Three weeks into my church study group on Christian disciplines, I introduced the members to fasting as an important component of prayer life. Then I gave practical instructions so that they could try fasting during the week and return with stories of their experiences.

When we gathered again, I could hardly wait to hear their accounts of the heavens opening up, of burning bushes and flashes of lightning, or at least stories of a still, small voice. The first person to speak said, 'I just felt hungry.' Her honesty rattled me and deflated my enthusiasm. Not one person in the group reported a 'mountaintop experience'. Our experiment with fasting had failed – or so I thought.

When I had recovered from my disappointment, I discovered a beautiful truth about fasting. By fasting, we demonstrate our love for Christ in a very tangible way. We practise honouring God over our own passions and desires. For a short period of time, we choose not to eat because following the way of Christ is more important than our appetites as we pray, 'Not what I want, but what you want.'

The Christian journey rarely consists of burning bushes and lightning bolts. The euphoria, if it comes at all, is generally short-lived. Instead, we learn to value the way of Christ over our own ways. One mundane day at a time, we are being transformed into the image of Christ.

Prayer: *Dear Lord, throughout this day, help us to choose your way over ours. Amen*

Thought for the day: I can act on my faith regardless of how I feel.

Kevin Thomas (Alabama, US)

PRAYER FOCUS: THOSE STARTING A NEW SPIRITUAL PRACTICE

When we weep

Read Jeremiah 31:15–17

The Lord says: 'A voice is heard in Ramah, mourning and great weeping, Rachel weeping for her children and refusing to be comforted, because they are no more.'
Jeremiah 31:15 (NIV)

My son was just seven years old when he watched the news report on TV announcing that our country was going to war. His brother asked a couple of questions about war, and then they went off to play. That evening, when the seven-year-old went to bed, I heard him crying. When I asked what was wrong, he told me he was worried about the war. I explained that it was far, far away and that he would be safe. But he just sobbed more. As I held him, he calmed down and said, 'I am not worried for me, Mummy; I am worried about all the mummies crying!' It touched my heart to hear his words, and I was amazed at how far his thinking had gone. Of course, he was quite right – many mothers would be crying. So we prayed for them and for all who might be hurt by the war.

In today's passage from Jeremiah, we read that God hears our weeping and understands our sadness. He promises that those weeping for the lost will be comforted and promises us hope for the future. He is not distant or uncaring, but comforts and strengthens us in our grief.

Prayer: *God of comfort, be with all those who are weeping today. Hasten the day when war will be no more. Amen*

Thought for the day: When I weep, God offers me comfort and hope.

Pam Lewis (Essex, England)

Shadow of God's wings

Read Psalm 63:1–11

You have been my help, and in the shadow of your wings I sing for joy.
Psalm 63:7 (NRSV)

As I began my morning stroll, the Texas air was already heavy with humidity and hot from intense sunshine. Much of my route was in direct sunlight, and I found myself longing for the shade cast by the few trees lining the road. When I found some shade, the refreshment and coolness beckoned me to slow my pace.

As I strolled through one of the larger shadows, I heard a bird singing in the branches overhead. I thought of the verse quoted above: 'In the shadow of your wings I sing for joy.' Just as the bird sang joyfully from the shaded tree branches, I too was rejoicing in the shadow of the tree's protection from the heat as I continued my walk toward home.

When we are struggling, life can feel like the furnace of a hot summer. Yet in the shadow of God's wings we can grow in faith despite difficulties that threaten to overwhelm us. Through Christian fellowship, prayer and scripture, we can rejoice in God's goodness as we walk toward our heavenly home.

Prayer: *Father God, renew us in the shadow of your wings. Help us to abide in your presence through prayer and your word each day of our lives. Amen*

Thought for the day: In the shadow of God's presence, I can find refreshment.

Montra C. Weaver (Texas, US)

Wilderness experience

Read Matthew 4:1–11

Jesus answered [the tempter], 'It is written, "One does not live by bread alone, but by every word that comes from the mouth of God."'
Matthew 4:4 (NRSV)

Because I was unable to find work or somewhere to live after I left college, my life was uncertain. Then I reread Matthew's account of Jesus' struggle in the wilderness and my perspective changed. I began to see parallels between Jesus being tempted to satisfy his physical hunger and my own situation. The way Jesus overcame temptation showed me a way to resist my need to control what was happening to me.

My summer of uncertainty led me to consider what it meant for Jesus to be hungry. His response to temptation was simply that 'one does not live by bread alone'. Jesus was referring to the need for us to be hungry for God. By reclaiming my hunger for God, I was able better to appreciate that angels ministered to Jesus after his time of trial in the wilderness (Matthew 4:11).

I now realise that my Christian community became those angels to me, giving me sustenance and support. The more spiritually hungry I became, the more thankful I was for the grace they showed me. Today, whenever I face uncertainty, I am no longer overcome by panic. Instead, I view it as a time to draw closer to God and look for ways to minister to others.

Prayer: *Dear Lord, help us to hear our neighbours' cries of suffering. May we be witnesses to your mercy for everyone we encounter. Amen*

Thought for the day: In uncertain times, I can turn to God and to my community of faith.

Trevor B. Williams (Tennessee, US)

Just a prayer away

Read Jeremiah 29:10–14

The Lord says, 'You will call on me and come and pray to me, and I will listen to you.'
Jeremiah 29:12 (NIV)

One night I suddenly woke up at midnight and spent two hours trying to get back to sleep. Unresolved problems and burdens from the previous days preyed on my mind. Then I remembered something from one of my minister's sermons. He said, 'If any night you find you cannot sleep, pray. It is a privilege and gift to talk with God.'

In the silence of that night, I started to pray and tell God many things. It was very enjoyable. I talked about my family, friends, desires and plans. And when I told God about my problems and burdens, I felt as if all of them were gone. My heart felt light and filled with joy and peace.

I soon fell asleep again. When I woke up the next morning, I knew that I had experienced a very special and valuable moment when I realised how close God always is to me – just a prayer away.

Prayer: *Dear God, thank you for always hearing us when we pray and for being with us in every situation. We pray as your Son taught us, saying, 'Our Father which art in heaven, Hallowed be thy name. Thy kingdom come. Thy will be done in earth, as it is in heaven. Give us this day our daily bread. And forgive us our debts, as we forgive our debtors. And lead us not into temptation, but deliver us from evil: For thine is the kingdom, and the power, and the glory, for ever. Amen.'**

Thought for the day: Prayer can change everything.

Meliana Santoso (East Java, Indonesia)

PRAYER FOCUS: THOSE WHO HAVE TROUBLE SLEEPING
*Matthew 6:9–13, KJV

Blooming again

Read James 5:13–18

God will save you from the hunter's trap and from deadly sickness. God will protect you with his pinions; you'll find refuge under his wings.
Psalm 91:3–4 (CEB)

One hot and humid summer, we were away from home on a two-week trip. Before leaving, I had watered the plants, including two geraniums that were full of brilliant red blooms. We returned to find the geraniums with wilted leaves. The flowers that had survived were dull and their centre petals had shrivelled to a deep burgundy instead of being bright red. I was afraid that we might lose the plants completely. So I watered them and pruned away dead leaves and old blooms. Within a week, they were revived and blooming again.

Eight years before, after extensive surgery and six months of chemo and radiation therapy, I had felt like those geraniums. With a scarred body and spirit I was wilted and dulled, emotionally and physically. But I was kept alive by skilled surgeons, effective drugs, prayer and the care of hospital staff, family and friends.

Cancer-free now, I have a greater appreciation for each day and greater gratitude for the most important people and essential things in life. Because of those stressful and frightening experiences, I am ready to serve God more fully. Like the revived and flourishing geraniums, I have been able to put forth new blossoms of service and creativity.

Prayer: *Thank you, Lord, for your faithful presence through difficult times. Amen*

Thought for the day: Though I am weak, God is strong.

John R. Robinson (Ohio, US)

Boring faith?

Read 2 Timothy 3:14–17

Train children in the way they should go; when they grow old, they won't depart from it.
Proverbs 22:6 (CEB)

When I was a child, my father was adamant about regular family Bible study and prayer time. I just wanted to play outside, watch television or read mystery novels. One morning, the school bus driver arrived early and waited outside where, much to my embarrassment, our family of four was in full view through the living room window as we knelt in prayer. When we ran out to get on the bus, our friends asked my sister and me why we were all lined up in a row with our heads down. Afraid of being laughed at, we answered that we were helping our parents put a new cover on the living room sofa.

In my teenage years I would arrive home from my school activities to find my father sitting at his desk with a well-worn and marked-up Bible open before him. I would sigh and think that Dad was at it again. What a boring way to spend an evening!

Now with a family of my own, I think differently of my father's example as I delve into his old, tattered Bible. The inheritance of faith and Bible study my father left me gives me a sense of security that money can't buy, and I thank both of my parents for that legacy.

Prayer: *Dear Father, thank you for the spiritual leaders in our families and communities. Help us to pass on our faith to younger generations. Amen*

Thought for the day: How can I be a spiritual leader in my household?

Wilma R. Vernich (Tennessee, US)

Plodding along

Read Isaiah 40:25–31

Those who hope in the Lord will renew their strength. They will soar on wings like eagles; they will run and not grow weary, they will walk and not be faint.
Isaiah 40:31 (NIV)

In today's reading, I expect Isaiah to put the verbs in the order of walk, run, soar – to end his poem on a high point. However, Isaiah starts with soaring eagles and ends with the feebler verb, walk. Why does Isaiah start with the grand and end with the ordinary?

As I think about how I face challenges in my life, however, I take comfort in this reversed order. When I return from a spiritual retreat, I feel as if I can take on the world. I can meet challenges head-on and win. I am soaring like an eagle! Inevitably, though, life beats me down. I stop soaring, but I am still running. As I run, more obstacles slow my pace, and I am soon down to a walk. What does Isaiah mean by, 'they will walk and not be faint'? I think he means plodding along, taking challenges in my stride and facing the painful, the fatiguing and the boring without giving up.

Life is not always about soaring. Often, it's simply finding the strength to put one foot in front of the other when we'd rather not. We can look again at Isaiah's 'backward' sentence and take comfort!

Prayer: *Faithful God, help us to watch for others who need our encouragement. Amen*

Thought for the day: God will walk with me through life's highs and lows.

Tom Smith (Utah, US)

Unforeseen blessings

Read Lamentations 3:22–24

Certainly the faithful love of the Lord hasn't ended; certainly God's compassion isn't through!
Lamentations 3:22 (CEB)

At the end of a dry winter, we finally received about an inch and a half of rain. It was amazing how much fresher the garden looked. Everything was greener and stood taller. A few days later, I noticed dozens of small lettuce seedlings poking up between the brick paving which forms the garden path among our vegetable beds. Because the bricks had absorbed so much moisture from the rain, they were damp enough to encourage the growth of tiny self-sown lettuce seeds in a way which the soil struggled to do. Because of the dry year, I hadn't expected the lettuces to survive. But here they were, creating an amazing example of God's surprising abundance.

God's gifts don't always come neatly packaged, growing in tidy rows or in the 'right' places. From my experience of God's gifts in unforeseen and totally unexpected places, I have seen that he can always surprise and delight us.

Prayer: *Loving Father, thank you for surprising and delighting us with your bounty, just when we need it most. Amen*

Thought for the day: God has surprises in store for me each day.

Meg Mangan (New South Wales, Australia)

Heading heavenward

Read Genesis 12:1–10

[Abraham] looked for a city which hath foundations, whose builder and maker is God.
Hebrews 11:10 (KJV)

At God's call, Abraham and Sarah (then Abram and Sarai) left Ur, the city of their family. God had promised to make of Abraham a great nation, through which all the earth would be blessed. How Abraham must have questioned this as the years passed and Sarah remained barren! Yet when they both reached a very old age, Isaac was born to them – truly God's miracle and the beginning of God's people, the Israelites (see Genesis 21:2–5.) Through Abraham and Sarah, many generations later, would come the Saviour of the world (see Matthew 1:1–16.)

Two years ago when our family, consisting of our teenage grandson, our daughter, son-in-law, their infant son, my husband, myself, two cats and a turtle, bounced along the motorway in our two vehicles, I thought of Abraham's courage. Like Abraham, we were leaving a comfortable home for an unknown, far-away ministry with our eldest daughter and her family. Abraham trusted the Lord through the difficulties and uncertainties. We can look to Abraham's example of faith to propel us forward over the bumps of this challenging earthly life.

Prayer: *Dear Lord, help us look to you when we face uncertainties. Remind us that no matter where we move, our eternal home is with you. Amen*

Thought for the day: Day by day, through joy and tears, I will follow God.

Cynthia Losness (Michigan, US)

Mother's legacy

Read Psalm 146:1–10
I will praise the Lord all my life; I will sing praise to my God as long as I live.
Psalm 146:2 (NIV)

'Betty, you are my favourite patient!' the young doctor greeted my 90-year-old mother when my sister and I accompanied her to a regular check-up. Mum has been dealing with dementia for many years. The doctor asked her detailed questions to gauge her mental capacity. She had difficulty answering trivial questions, so the doctor asked, 'Betty, can you write a sentence or two?'

Without hesitation, Mum quickly wrote on a piece of paper, folded it, and handed it to the doctor. The doctor read aloud, 'Jesus said… "I am the way, and the truth, and the life. No one comes to the Father except through me"' (John 14:6, NRSV).

'Doctor, you can believe it!' Mum said, her face glowing. The doctor smiled as he completed his notes.

After the appointment, we took Mum back to her sheltered housing complex, where she is cherished by the staff and other residents as she shares God's love through her joyful spirit. We will never forget how Mum ended her prayer with us that day: 'Jesus, I hope you have a wonderful day!'

Despite her illness, Mum continues to be an example of God's faithfulness, inspiring us as she leaves her spiritual legacy. Her prayer reminded us that we can always talk to Jesus as a friend.

Prayer: *Dear Jesus, thank you for your faithfulness, and thank you for being a friend to us. Amen*

Thought for the day: Jesus is my Saviour and my friend.

Susan Bates (Oregon, US)

A rich harvest

Read Matthew 13:1–23

The seed falling on good soil refers to someone who hears the word and understands it. This is the one who produces a crop, yielding a hundred, sixty or thirty times what was sown.
Matthew 13:23 (NIV)

One of our church members invited us to her farm to have a go at growing food. We got up early one day to plant taros, a type of root vegetable. Several weeks later, we were invited back to check each taro we had planted and remove weeds around it to help it grow healthily and to obtain a rich harvest. We found that every young taro looked bigger than before, which made us happy. However, when we looked carefully, we saw that almost every taro had been surrounded by weeds; some of the weeds had even grown bigger than the taros. We started to pull out the weeds from around the taros. One of my church members advised me as she watched my work, 'Just picking the weeds is not enough. You have to pull out the roots!'

This experience made me think about our spiritual growth as Christians. We can cultivate spiritual fruit: love, joy, peace, patience, kindness, goodness, faithfulness, gentleness and self-control. To make this possible, we must completely remove all the weeds – including the roots – that hinder our spiritual growth.

Prayer: *Dear God, help us to remove what is unnecessary in our lives in order to be what you want us to be. Amen*

Thought for the day: What 'weeds' are hindering my spiritual growth?

Kazuo Ishikawa (Akita, Japan)

The lonely lamb

Read Psalm 23

He tends his flock like a shepherd: he gathers the lambs in his arms and carries them close to his heart.
Isaiah 40:11 (NIV)

Driving out of the estate where we had been on holiday, we noticed a single lamb at the edge of the field. It was obviously some days since his birth; his legs were strong, but it was surprising to see him there all alone. All week we had enjoyed watching the flocks of ewes with their newborn lambs, gambling around or sucking contentedly.

I suddenly caught a glimpse of the shepherd in the field. He had a tiny lamb in his arms, probably destined for the warmth of the farmhouse until it was stronger. But he had also spotted the wanderer and was now striding purposefully towards it. This lone lamb was not in need of warmth or shelter, but it needed to be sent back in the right direction, to be reunited with its mother and be kept safe and protected.

How comforting it is to know that, though we may have walked for a long time with Jesus, when we are prone to wander, he will meet us and bring us back to where we need to be.

Prayer: *Thank you, Lord, for seeking and saving us when we stray from you. Help us to remember that we can never wander beyond your love and care. Amen*

Thought for the day: Jesus is the Good Shepherd who is always with us.

Pauline Lewis (South Wales)

Losses

Read Psalm 84

[The Lord] put a new song in my mouth, a song of praise to our God. Many will see and fear, and put their trust in the Lord.
Psalm 40:3 (NRSV)

One day while having my hair cut, the new stylist told me about her experience with chemotherapy. She spoke of fear, hospital visits, feelings of anger and despair. When her treatment ended, she began to heal physically and emotionally. And that summer, she planted a garden. She said, 'I knew nothing about gardening, but it was good therapy. When my tomato plants bloomed, I was so happy; but when the blooms withered, I cried, not realising that small tomatoes were beginning to grow. When they grew and ripened, we had homemade salsa all summer.'

Her words made me think of losses in our lives. When we're young, it is easy to focus on hopes and plans; but later, we begin to lose one thing after another. Children grow up and leave home, jobs end, health fails, we lose friends. Eventually, we feel as if we have nothing left to lose. In time, however, we begin to see that God often replaces a loss with something new and unexpected: a friend who holds us up, a new interest to replace what we can no longer do, or perhaps compassion for others we would not have had without the loss. Loss is not God's final word.

Prayer: *Thank you, God, for your love, which will never let us down and gives us hope wherever life takes us. Amen*

Thought for the day: When I feel overwhelmed by loss, I will look for what God is growing in me.

Eleanor Cowles (Oregon, US)

Late to church

Read Galatians 6:1–10

Carry each other's burdens, and in this way you will fulfil the law of Christ.
Galatians 6:2 (NIV)

One Sunday I was running late for the morning church service, so I decided to take a taxi to get there as quickly as possible. A woman and I hailed the same taxi. I had waved my hand first, so the taxi came to a stop near me. The woman came over and said, 'Sir, my daughter is not well. She has had a major heart attack and has been rushed to hospital.' It was raining that day and there were no other means of transport. My heart was filled with pity for her. I got out of the taxi and offered it to her.

I arrived at church late that day, but my heart was full of a deep sense of satisfaction and peace of mind that I had helped someone that day. After all, this is what God requires us to do as followers of Christ. We carry his cross every day so that we can bear one another's burdens and reflect Christ's light to others, so that they may be blessed.

Prayer: *Dear Lord, help us to bear one another's burdens as you have borne ours. Amen*

Thought for the day: How can I share the light of Christ today?

Jai Knox (Uttar Pradesh, India)

Lollipop lesson

Read Luke 15:11–21

Thy kingdom come. Thy will be done in earth, as it is in heaven.
Matthew 6:10 (KJV)

During my childhood, my mother and I would often pass the sweet counter in a certain department store. Each time, I asked for one of the enticing lollipops that were six inches in diameter. After repeated denials, my mother relented one day and bought me one. At first, I was thrilled. However, as the afternoon wore on, I got tired of holding the wooden stick with its heavy load of sticky sweet. Mother warned me that if I put it down, it would get dirty and I would have to throw it away. That's how I learned that getting what I thought I wanted wasn't necessarily a good thing.

The Bible shows us several people who wanted something that turned out not to be such a good thing. For example, the prodigal son wanted his inheritance before his father died. After spending his money extravagantly, he ended up impoverished and hungry. I often wondered why his father agreed to give his son his inheritance, but maybe it was the same lesson my mother taught me when she bought me the huge lollipop. At times, God seems to teach that lesson, too. I've learned that it's important to end my prayer requests with, 'Your will be done.' God knows what is best for me.

Prayer: *Dear Lord, thank you for caring for us enough to say, 'No'. Amen*

Thought for the day: God loves me enough to say, 'No' and lead me in a new direction.

Mary Hunt Webb (New Mexico, US)

One page at a time

Read Psalm 119:105–112
Your word is a lamp for my feet, a light on my path.
Psalm 119:105 (NIV)

When I first became a Christian, I wanted to read the Bible from cover to cover, but that seemed like a daunting task. Then, when I realised that the Bible is one large book which has been organised into smaller books, it seemed a lot easier. If I were to read only one page per day in my Bible, I could read through the Bible in less than three years. If I were to read three pages per day, it would take less than a year.

Nothing else we could read is as important or beneficial to our lives as the Bible – God's gift to us. In it, the mind of God is revealed to us. It contains everything we need to know about living a life that pleases him. It will guide us through even the darkest times. The more thoroughly and intently we read the Bible, the more completely we will come to know God.

At first reading the whole Bible may seem almost impossible, but the rewards are well worth our time and effort. Whether it's a verse, a chapter or a book – reading the Bible every day will equip us to serve God fully.

Prayer: *Gracious God, thank you for revealing yourself to us through your word. By your Holy Spirit, help us to read and to understand it. Amen*

Thought for the day: I will discover something new in God's word today.

Steven Cohen (California, US)

Overwhelmed and amazed

Read Mark 7:31–37

People were overwhelmed with amazement. 'He has done everything well,' they said.
Mark 7:37 (NIV)

Although the people in today's reading had begged Jesus to heal the man who was deaf and had difficulty speaking, they were still amazed when God granted their request. Even though the man had been suffering for a long time, he didn't complain, 'What took you so long?' Perhaps the man's long years of suffering intensified the amazement of the onlookers.

I can relate to this story because God once healed me. I had endured over a decade of heartbreaking infertility. And when my husband and I attempted to adopt, the birth mother changed her mind and kept her child. Then, a few weeks after our twelfth wedding anniversary, I gave birth to our son. I, too, was 'overwhelmed with amazement' at God's power. I most certainly didn't ask the Lord what took so long as I cuddled my baby against my skin and marvelled at each and every one of his fingers and toes. Instead, I rejoiced so exuberantly that the nurse remarked about the intensity of my happiness.

Whenever I'm begging Jesus to address my concerns, I remember that wonderful answer to prayer, and I focus on God's ability to do all things well in his time.

Prayer: *Dear Lord, help us to wait patiently and expectantly as we come to you with our concerns. Amen*

Thought for the day: When I want to give up hope, God can amaze me.

Wendy L. Macdonald (British Columbia, Canada)

PRAYER FOCUS: SOMEONE STRUGGLING WITH INFERTILITY   27

Imitator

Read Hebrews 13:1–8

Remember your leaders, who spoke the word of God to you. Consider the outcome of their way of life and imitate their faith.
Hebrews 13:7 (NIV)

The days leading up to my father's funeral were a mixture of sorrow and beauty. I had time to spend with family and the opportunity to reconnect with old friends. We recalled stories of Dad, laughing at some and crying at others. We felt an incredible, and often unexplainable, sense of joy and peace. While we greatly missed Dad, we knew that he was with his heavenly Father even while we mourned.

In one of our conversations, my sister said that she could see a little bit of my father's personality and character in each of his grandchildren. The eldest grandson demonstrates my father's loyalty to family and friends. My niece possesses Dad's easy-going approach to life. My daughter is blessed with a spirit of quiet contemplation, while my son has a fund of one-liners. Each of these characteristics was evident often during my father's lifetime and is carried on in the lives of his grandchildren.

Scripture calls us to imitate those who have gone before us in the Christian faith, to follow their example of obedience, perseverance, joy and love. I know that my father was not perfect, but Dad trusted Jesus to forgive his shortcomings and to love him in spite of them. That kind of faith and trust is certainly worth imitating.

Prayer: *Dear God, thank you for leaders in the faith who are with us now and for those who have gone ahead of us. Help us to imitate their lives of faith. In Jesus' name. Amen*

Thought for the day: I will imitate the faith of those who have gone before me.

Chuck Kralik (Missouri, US)

A heavenly home

Read John 14:1–6

Jesus said, 'My Father's house has many rooms... if I go and prepare a place for you, I will come back and take you to be with me that you also may be where I am.'
John 14:2–3 (NIV)

When I was pregnant for the first time, I was so excited to become a mother. I spent hours decorating the baby's room in anticipation of his arrival. My husband and I painted the walls, picked out furniture, and purchased the special touches to prepare the nursery for our son's homecoming. As I tucked tiny T-shirts and little socks into the chest of drawers, I would imagine what he would look like and how sweet it would be to hold him in my arms. Sitting in the rocking chair in his nursery, I would look around and smile at what we had lovingly prepared for the arrival of our son. I was filled with excitement and anticipation.

Just as a new mother looks forward to the day that she will bring her baby home, Jesus is planning to come back for us and take us to his Father's house where he has lovingly prepared a room for us. He wants to spend time with us and is excited about our arrival.

In the meantime, we can eagerly and prayerfully await his return, when he will take us to our heavenly home. The thought of a room prepared by the Saviour himself is enough to make me smile and fill me with excitement and anticipation.

Prayer: *Dear Saviour, thank you for lovingly preparing a place for us in your Father's house. Help us to follow you as we await your return. Amen*

Thought for the day: Jesus is preparing a room for me.

Sarah Lyons (Kansas, US)

Power of forgiveness

Read Genesis 18:23–33

Peter came to Jesus and asked, 'Lord, how many times shall I forgive my brother or sister who sins against me? Up to seven times?' Jesus answered, 'I tell you, not seven times, but seventy-seven times.'
Matthew 18:21–22 (NIV)

Within a month of my starting to attend church, a friend invited me to participate in a church-sponsored event called 'Encounter with Christ'. At the event today's reading and quoted verse had a profound impact on me. After the event, I telephoned my son's mother. Since our separation we had not been able to hold a civil conversation for more than five minutes. But after the lessons I learned at the church event, everything changed. I asked for her forgiveness for all of my deplorable behaviour that I could recall and for all the things I could not recall as well. We spoke for 45 minutes.

Since that day, I have felt great relief from a burden that I had not realised was weighing so heavily on me: the absence of forgiveness. Today, my son's mother and I share a beautiful relationship – one that is only possible through Christ when we make him our priority in all things.

Prayer: *Creator God, thank you for teaching us about forgiveness, love, mercy and generosity. In the name of Jesus we pray. Amen*

Thought for the day: Forgiveness can transform my relationship with God and others.

John W. Garcia M. (Cali, Colombia)

Even stronger now

Read Joshua 1:1–18

Be strong and courageous. Do not be afraid; do not be discouraged, for the Lord your God will be with you wherever you go.
Joshua 1:9 (NIV)

A few years ago, I was diagnosed with breast cancer and had to undergo chemotherapy and several operations. During this time, my position at work was terminated and my husband lost his job. I remember thinking, how can this be? This too, when we're feeling so vulnerable? However, though it was a very difficult time, it was also a time of great joy because my younger daughter graduated from university and my older daughter got married. Throughout all of this, I prayed and asked God to allow me time to grow old with my husband, see my daughters reach their goals, and hopefully enjoy grandchildren someday. As I prayed, I felt the warmth and peace of the Holy Spirit.

Three months after my diagnosis, my husband got a new job; and at the end of my treatment I was offered a new and exciting position. To this day, my check-ups with my oncologist show no signs of cancerous cells. My daughters are well on their way to fulfilling their goals, and my husband and I are blessed with a grandson!

Just as God commanded Joshua not to be afraid or discouraged, God encouraged me. My faith is even stronger now because I know that the Lord is with me no matter what challenges I may face.

Prayer: *Dear Father, thank you for the gift of life. Help us to appreciate each and every day. Amen*

Thought for the day: I can have courage because God is always with me.

Blanca Longhurst (Tennessee, US)

PRAYER FOCUS: THOSE UNDERGOING CANCER TREATMENT

The sudden storm

Read Psalm 46:1–7

We will not fear... though [the sea's] waters roar and foam.
Psalm 46:2–3 (NIV)

My bass-fishing partner and I were enjoying a good catch on the lake. The weather had been perfect until a fierce storm blew up rather quickly, so we quickly stowed our gear, then ran the boat at full speed in the rain to find a place where we would be safe and secure.

Just in time, we spotted an empty, covered boat jetty at the back of a small cove just off the creek channel, where we could tie up the boat. The jetty became our refuge while the storm raged.

The rain came so heavily and so fast that we could see a foaming stream of run-off rushing in the main channel about two feet above the level of the water. The power of the stream surely would have swamped our boat. We learned later that a tornado had touched down nearby.

As I reflect on that day, I remember those times when the storms of life arise, often without warning. These storms can frighten us with their challenges and interrupt our dreams.

But just as the boat jetty offered shelter from the thunderstorm, we can find shelter in the arms and protection of God. What comfort to know that God hears our prayers and is working for good in all the circumstances of our lives!

Prayer: *Almighty and loving God, thank you for hearing our prayers and for giving us refuge, security and peace. In Jesus' name. Amen*

Thought for the day: I can always find refuge in God's loving arms.

Bob Peterson (Texas, US)

A plank in my eye

Read Matthew 7:1–5

Why do you look at the speck of sawdust in your brother's eye and pay no attention to the plank in your own eye?
Matthew 7:3 (NIV)

For years, my husband and I shared the wash-basin in our bathroom. Spots of toothpaste were always on the taps – the spots put there, I was certain, by my husband. And it was a constant irritation to me. I would see the marks and think, 'Why can't he clean up after himself?' or just be plain mad at his sloppiness. A few months ago we moved into a new house with two basins in the master bathroom. One day I realised that my husband's sink and taps were clean. Mine were covered with spots of toothpaste. What a revelation that was, and what an embarrassment to me!

This realisation caused me to reflect on the Bible verse quoted above. It is so easy for us to assume that we are perfect and to be critical of everyone else. Jesus didn't see people that way. He challenged us to examine our own flaws and to work to correct them according to God's will.

Prayer: *Dear Father, help us to be aware of our failings and to be gentle with ourselves and others. As Jesus taught us, we pray, 'Father, hallowed be your name, your kingdom come. Give us each day our daily bread. Forgive us our sins, for we also forgive everyone who sins against us. And lead us not into temptation.'* Amen*

Thought for the day: When I am tempted to judge others, God can help me reflect on my own faults.

Martha Swann Murphy-Shipley (South Carolina, US)

A little beyond

Read 1 Peter 5:6–11

Resist [the devil], steadfast in your faith, for you know that your brothers and sisters in all the world are undergoing the same kinds of suffering.
1 Peter 5:9 (NRSV)

I enjoy exercising by attending an aerobic dance class. The instructor shouts words of encouragement from her place in the front. With an elastic band held in each of my hands stretched out in front of me, I hear her say, 'Try to stretch the band as far as you can and then a little beyond. If you expect to get stronger, you need to meet and exceed the resistance!'

Later I realised that these words apply to my faith life as well. As I identify areas of challenge, I now see them differently. Perhaps God is calling me to cultivate character traits like patience, acceptance and kindness. I've found that those traits are easy to reflect when I'm around loved ones and friends but much harder when I'm surrounded by people who seem different from me. I am challenged now to find those areas where I 'resist' treating others the way Christ would and then push past this resistance. When I went to the gym to work out my body, God helped me to work on my spirit as well.

Prayer: *Dear God, help us to trust in you, and train us to reflect your glory in all that we do. Amen*

Thought for the day: Where is God asking me to stretch beyond my routine?

Connie Schroeder (California, US)

Spiritual reserves

Read Jeremiah 17:5–8

The one who trusts in the Lord, whose confidence is in him... will be like a tree planted by the water that sends out its roots by the stream.
Jeremiah 17:7–8 (NIV)

It was one of those days when nothing seemed to go right. Milk boiled over. The dog went missing, and I was late for an appointment because the car wouldn't start. The local garage was closed. Who would help? The saving grace in all this was that I could draw on the memory of God's actions in the past, times when he had rescued me from more than one predicament and faith had sustained me.

In today's reading, Jeremiah gave the people of Judah sound advice: stay close to God in good times, and – like a tree planted by a stream – store up the sustenance needed for times of drought. In a land of low rainfall, the indigenous trees send their roots down deep to where the water is stored and thus most survive even the worst droughts.

It's so easy to have 'spiritual amnesia' when life is going well. Maintaining a deep relationship with God during the good times sustains us during the bad times. Because of God's actions in the past, we can be certain of his faithfulness in the future.

Prayer: *O God, give us the right words to share our faith with someone we meet today so that they can know your love and grace. Amen*

Thought for the day: I can drink deeply from my spiritual reserve of faith in God.

Linda Sutton (South Australia, Australia)

Lending kindness

Read Matthew 5:1–12

Whoever is kind to the poor lends to the Lord, and will be repaid in full.
Proverbs 19:17 (NRSV)

Recently I had a terrible cold. My throat was sore, I was aching, feeling run down, and my nose was running. I had no medicine so I decided to get some fresh air on the prison exercise yard. While I was on my walk, an inmate I hardly knew asked how I was doing and offered me some cough sweets and some tissues. He wanted nothing in return. He could see my discomfort and thought only of how he could help. Later that evening a friend offered me more cough sweets. I soon began to feel much better in body and spirit thanks to the kindness and caring of those two fellow inmates.

Although I am in prison, I see acts of kindness, sharing and giving every day. In my unit alone there are two 'love boxes' – collection boxes for donations such as toiletries for the inmates who cannot afford to buy these things for themselves. The true spirit of charity is one of the greatest things I have become part of and witnessed while in prison – people placing the needs of others before their own. From simple acts of kindness to an entire inmate population helping one another, it's a beautiful thing to witness. God invites all of us to do the same.

Prayer: *Dear God, teach us to care for others the way you care for us. Amen*

Thought for the day: To whom can I show God's love through an act of kindness?

Christopher Hill (Michigan, US)

A way of life

Read Luke 11:1–13
Pray without ceasing.
1 Thessalonians 5:17 (KJV)

In the spring of 2002 I was trying to find my way back to God. Having planted about ten Busy Lizzie plants around our hickory tree, I used my plant-watering time as an opportunity to pray for family and close friends. Each plant represented a person, and I kidded our daughter that her flowers were the largest and most beautiful.

Something as simple as watering plants became a time to both talk and listen to God. For me it was an eagerly awaited, peaceful time. It led to prayer times indoors on rainy days. Gradually, prayer has become a regular part of my morning routine regardless of the weather. It is easy to be thankful during the early spring and summer sunrises that give me so much joy. But my joy carries over to the grey days as well, when I find just as much to be thankful for.

My plant-watering prayer time has led me to pray throughout the day – when I seek special guidance or want to give thanks for the times when God's guidance upheld me in difficult situations. Prayer has indeed led me back to God and has become for me a way of life.

Prayer: *Dear God, direct us to find times to communicate with you. Help us to listen for your wisdom and guidance. Amen*

Thought for the day: A simple prayer can open my life to God's presence.

Linda Kinde (Ohio, US)

Quite a climb

Read Philippians 2:1–11

Be perfect, therefore, as your heavenly Father is perfect.
Matthew 5:48 (NRSV)

On a recent holiday I took two of my sons to northern New Mexico where we saw many beautiful places and visited a number of historic sites. We also spent one day climbing Wheeler Peak, the highest mountain in the state. I had been exercising and losing weight in anticipation of this great adventure, but I knew that the real challenge was going to be the thin air. Wheeler Peak is 13,160 feet high.

As I slowly made my way up the mountain, I began to think, 'Am I willing to exert this much effort in my walk with God? Am I as determined to reach the pinnacle of faith as I am to reach the pinnacle of this mountain?' Though I had to stop quite often to catch my breath, I made it to the top.

At times I thought about giving up the climb, but I did not entertain those thoughts for long. I had come too far and worked too hard to give up. So, am I that committed to pushing the limits of my love for Christ and my neighbours? I may not be a great mountain climber, but I am trying to be a 'spiritual giant'. I want to go as far and as high as Christ will take me, because he is the pioneer and perfecter of my faith (see Hebrews 12:2).

Prayer: *Dear Lord, help us to give our best efforts in deepening our relationship with you. Help us to love our neighbours as we love ourselves. Amen*

Thought for the day: How much effort am I giving in my walk with God?

Michael L. Fraley (Texas, US)

Caring for creation

Read Psalm 104:10–28

Look at the birds of the air; they do not sow or reap or store away in barns, and yet your heavenly Father feeds them.
Matthew 6:26 (NIV)

One Sunday morning I found myself looking out at the back garden, which was cloaked in a layer of snow. As I stood enjoying the beautiful wintry scene, I noticed that a large tree had dropped its tiny cones – delivering seeds to the ground where rabbits, squirrels and birds delighted in nature's gift to them.

After church, I again stopped to take in the snowy landscape that always draws my heart and mind to God and creation. A fresh layer of snow had fallen, and on top of the snow lay more tiny cones. It was as if God had shaken the tree branches to provide more food for the animals. The scene was a perfect image of the verse from Matthew above. I smiled as I thought of the satisfaction I get from putting out bird seed and water all year around. I am God's hands and feet caring for creation, fulfilling the role I believe he plans for us all.

Watching the wildlife in my garden, I'm envious of their carefree nature. Truly they neither sow nor reap; nor do they worry. God feeds them – both directly through nature and indirectly through people like you and me who derive satisfaction from caring for his creatures, great and small.

Prayer: *Heavenly Father, thank you for the privilege of caring for your creation. Amen*

Thought for the day: Loving God means loving what he has created.

Nancy Allman-Bull (Ohio, US)

The best legacy

Read Deuteronomy 11:18–21

Fix these words of mine in your hearts and minds; tie them as symbols on your hands and bind them on your foreheads.
Deuteronomy 11:18 (NIV)

When I was a child, my father would gather the whole family together every evening to read the Bible and *The Upper Room*. When we prayed together and he gave a brief explanation of the scripture, I felt it come alive.

When I went to college, we had difficulty getting the family together. But I felt I was missing something if I skipped a day of the habit my father had instilled in us. So I subscribed to *The Upper Room*. I have read it every day since. The meditations guide me or remind me to begin the day with a peaceful mind.

Hours before Dad passed away in May 2013 he told us that even though he must leave us, we can keep in mind that God, our eternal Father, will never leave us. Things have never been the same since Dad died, but I keep his legacy of faith in God as our eternal Father in my heart. I pray to God in my ups and downs, in daily life and in nights full of tears. I seek God's word by reading the Bible every morning for strength.

I thank God for my dad and his legacy. When I have children, I will do the same to share the gift of God's eternal love.

Prayer: *God Almighty, thank you for good role models who show us how to follow you. Amen*

Thought for the day: What spiritual legacy will I leave?

Juita Kartini (Jakarta, Indonesia)

Mountains of air

Read Psalm 16:1–11

Can any of you by worrying add a single hour to your span of life?
Matthew 6:27 (NRSV)

Are my eyes playing tricks on me? Mountains that looked just like the ones I had left behind in Pennsylvania seemed to fill the horizon as I drove down an unfamiliar country road. All I could think of were long, winding roads ahead of me filled with steep slopes or maybe miles of backtracking around the foothills. That was definitely not what I wanted to see.

My new life in Michigan was struggle enough – what with trying to find a new job, a new church, new friends, a new doctor and new connections in the community. The last thing I needed was another mountain to climb, real or figurative. Then I took another look. What I thought were mountains were actually peaks of mist rising from Lake Michigan. As I drove toward them, they began to vanish; they were airy and without substance. My fears had transformed them into a threat.

How many times in my life have I worried about challenges that lay ahead, only to find that they weren't so difficult after all? And even when they were real, wasn't God's love sufficient to conquer them? 'Keep your eyes on the Lord,' I whispered to myself, 'and you will find strength to make the rough places a plain' (see Isaiah 40:3–5).

Prayer: *Dear Lord, when we feel overwhelmed by life's demands, help us to remember that you are always with us. Amen*

Thought for the day: Today and every day I can give my worries to the Lord.

Nancy Clark (Michigan, US)

Going forward in faith

Read Luke 5:1–11

Simon answered, 'Master, we have worked all night long but have caught nothing. Yet if you say so, I will let down the nets.'
Luke 5:5 (NRSV)

Our church recently lost one of its long-serving members. Over the course of her long life, Liz was an important mentor to many in our church. Many years ago, shortly after we had joined the church, Liz approached me about becoming the chair of the stewardship committee. I wasn't sure I was qualified, so I told her I would like to think about the offer. However, shortly after the conversation, our minister contacted me and thanked me for accepting the position.

In hindsight, Liz did me a big favour, because the position forced me to step out of my comfort zone. That first step of faith started my active service to the church that continues to this day. I know my faith has grown because of the opportunities I've had to serve, and I can thank Liz for getting me started.

When we receive an opportunity to serve the Lord, it may feel as if it is beyond our abilities. Or perhaps the call doesn't make sense to us. That was the case in today's scripture reading. Peter had much more experience of fishing than Jesus did. He had just spent all night fishing with no results when Jesus told him to put his nets out in deep water. But Peter did what Jesus asked. Peter not only caught nets full of fish, but he also took his first step toward a life of incredible faith. Stepping forward in faith, even when we have doubts, helps us to grow as followers of Christ.

Prayer: *Dear God, help me to step out in faith when you call me to serve. Amen*

Thought for the day: How is God asking me to step out of my comfort zone?

John D. Bown (Minnesota, US)

That peaceful hour

Read Psalm 139:1–10

In the morning, Lord, you hear my voice; in the morning I lay my requests before you and wait expectantly.
Psalm 5:3 (NIV)

Recently I read a report claiming that getting up an hour early, taking things slowly, and having a good breakfast is the best way to begin the day. Starting the day in a rush can cause stress levels to rise.

I find that spending time with God in the morning sets me right for the rest of the day. As the day proceeds, other demands rush in. Family needs surface, and my mind can become cluttered. Spending time in quiet contemplation, reading God's word and praying helps us to set the tone for the hours that follow. We can talk to God about any decisions we know we will be facing that day and then have time to wait for his response and guidance. We can pray for people who are weighing heavily on our hearts. Above all, we can spend time in thanksgiving and praise. No matter when it occurs in the day, a peaceful hour can be invaluable to our Christian life and spiritual growth.

Prayer: *O timeless God, thank you that our days can begin with you, continue with you and end with you. Amen*

Thought for the day: Time spent with God is time well spent.

Carol Purves (Cumbria, England)

Multiply my efforts!

Read Luke 9:12–17

[Jesus] said to [the disciples], 'You give them something to eat.' They said, 'We have no more than five loaves and two fish... for all these people.'
Luke 9:13 (NRSV)

I work as a spiritual director and youth minister. After days of working long hours to prepare for a youth retreat without asking for help, I finally prayed. 'God, I want to lead these young people to you, but I am completely exhausted. Please, multiply my efforts as you multiplied the loaves!'

Then I began to notice all the ways God was multiplying my efforts. Two days before the retreat, when it was time to pack my car with all the supplies and food for the weekend, I prayed for help. Moments later, the retreat leaders arrived for their meeting and asked if I needed anything. The day before the retreat, God helped me prioritise what needed to be done and what details I could let go. Then, throughout the retreat, volunteers came and took care of everything I was too exhausted to do.

The story in today's reading shows that God can take whatever we have – no matter how small the amount, how weak we feel, how poor, or how untalented we may be – and multiply it. When we seek God's will, we can trust that he is already working. We need only ask for his help.

Prayer: *Dear God, multiply our efforts as you multiplied the loaves and fishes! Amen*

Thought for the day: God will multiply my efforts.

Carrell Jamilano (California, US)

Trust and act

Read Matthew 25:35–40
Faith by itself, if it is not accompanied by action, is dead.
James 2:17 (NIV)

After descending the steps of the small plane at a rural airport, I walked into the terminal building, which looked more like a bus station than an airport. I picked up a courtesy phone, seeking to find a taxi into town to make a business appointment. The man on the phone said he could not drive me at the moment but suggested I go to the rental-car counter.

When I got there, I saw only another courtesy phone. Lifting it, I immediately recognised the voice. It was the same man! He told me to walk behind the counter. He then proceeded to give me the combination to the safe. He said I should feel free to take a set of keys and return the car when I had finished my business trip. I asked if he needed any credit card info or paperwork signed. He said no and then said, 'Welcome to Garden City; we trust people here.'

This man had extended to me extreme kindness and trust. His actions challenged me to be more kind and generous toward others. This experience reminded me that God doesn't care about the 'paperwork' but about our actions – acts of love that draw others into wanting to know more about the Christ we serve, the one in whom we can always trust.

Prayer: *Dear Lord, help us to share your kindness and love with others, especially when they do not expect it. Amen*

Thought for the day: How will I demonstrate God's grace through loving actions?

Larry Scanlan (Maryland, US)

The body of Christ

Read Hebrews 10:19–25
You are the body of Christ, and each one of you is a part of it.
1 Corinthians 12:27 (NIV)

I am part of an interdenominational Bible study. Every week over 300 women gather together to worship, discuss questions, hear a lecture on that week's reading, and pray. We represent every Christian denomination in our area. It doesn't matter if we belong to the biggest or the smallest church; we are all seeking to know more about the Bible and God, and to carry what we learn with us as we each go back to our own churches.

To me, this is what the body of Christ is all about: believers coming together to be enriched spiritually so that we can be the hands, feet, eyes, ears and mouth of Christ in our communities. Each week when we meet I imagine that God is smiling because we are functioning as one.

Prayer: *Dear Lord Jesus, thank you for the opportunity to be part of your body here on earth. We pray as you taught us saying, 'Our Father which art in heaven, Hallowed be thy name. Thy kingdom come. Thy will be done, as in heaven, so in earth. Give us day by day our daily bread. And forgive us our sins; for we also forgive every one that is indebted to us. And lead us not into temptation; but deliver us from evil.'* Amen*

Thought for the day: Every believer is part of the body of Christ.

Carol Denereaz (Victoria, Australia)

Daytime moon

Read Psalm 121:1–8

The Lord will watch over your coming and going both now and for evermore.
Psalm 121:8 (NIV)

As with most people I know, my life is a constant whirlwind. My days are filled with household duties, my job, my family, my friends and various other obligations. I sometimes feel overwhelmed by it all. But then, when I make the effort to slow down and notice the beauty of God's creation, I remember how his presence and peace can so readily surround me.

I am blessed to live in a beautiful mountainous place that I enjoy exploring when I hike with my happy, energetic dog. One day, I noticed the moon in the daytime sky – though I had to look carefully to see it. I started thinking: the moon is always there, whether we can see it or not. So it is with our God who is always here, watching over us, even when we do not particularly feel his presence.

Since that day, I often notice the moon in the daytime sky. It also seems that I see it more often when I'm feeling stressed, worried or sad. This became a reminder for me that God watches over me. It brings me comfort and peace and always makes me smile. Our loving God is here for us all, at this moment and always.

Prayer: *Dear God, show us signs of your love today, and help us to see them. Amen*

Thought for the day: Today I will look for signs of God's love and protection.

Tracy Morgan (Nevada, US)

No limits

Read Ephesians 4:4–10

Seek first [your heavenly Father's] kingdom and his righteousness, and all these things will be given to you as well.
Matthew 6:33 (NIV)

Jacob had been wearing the same pair of shoes for five years, and they were literally disintegrating on his feet. Though there are roughly 140 of us at this prison, death row has only twelve jobs available, each paying $2.80 per week. A pair of shoes costs $40.00, and Jacob is unemployed.

Recently, Jacob needed to leave the prison to see a doctor. While Jacob was waiting to go out, another prisoner being transferred to a different prison put a brand new pair of shoes on the counter and said, 'Give these to someone who needs them.' Technically, the officer was supposed to throw them away because prisoners are not allowed to give other prisoners gifts, but she felt moved to ask Jacob his shoe size. The shoes were a perfect fit. Jacob had been praying for God to provide for him and trusted that God would. Sometimes we put limits on what God can do because we focus on the 'normal' sources from which our needs are met. But God is limitless and can meet our needs in unexpected ways.

Prayer: *Dear God, help us to trust you to provide for our needs. Amen*

Thought for the day: With God there are no limits.

George T. Wilkerson (North Carolina, US)

God knows best

Read Isaiah 48:12–19

I am the Lord your God, who teaches you what is best for you, who directs you in the way you should go.
Isaiah 48:17 (NIV)

When our son Joel was learning to ride a bike, he had to ride in the driveway and on the lawn because there were no pavements near our house. Our gravel driveway was short and bumpy, and riding on the lawn wasn't much fun either. So Joel eyed the road in front of our house hopefully. My husband looked at the same road, but where Joel saw a straight, smooth, wide stretch where he could ride, my husband saw fast-moving traffic – definitely not a safe place for a five-year-old to develop his cycling skills. My husband didn't enjoy withholding this pleasure from our son, but where Joel saw fun, my husband saw danger.

Sometimes it is hard to understand God's commandments or why he withholds what looks so good and right to us. But our perspective is limited. We can't know or see what God knows and sees. We can only trust that out of great love for us, God looks out for our welfare to accomplish what is best for us in the long run.

Prayer: *Thank you, Father, for looking out for our good. Increase our trust in your loving heart. Amen*

Thought for the day: God knows best – better than I do.

Esther Zeiset (Pennsylvania, US)

Awakening to love

Read Psalm 52:8–9

I am convinced that neither death nor life... neither height nor depth, nor anything else in all creation, will be able to separate us from the love of God that is in Christ Jesus our Lord.
Romans 8:38–39 (NIV)

When my son was murdered three days before Christmas in 2014, my grief and depression became unbearable. I started questioning God's love for me and for my son. I just couldn't find any peace or comfort.

Mother's Day 2016 brought a remarkable change to my life. Even though I didn't want to, I went to church that day. When I arrived, my friends greeted me with hugs. During the children's talk, each child received a flower to give to a woman in the congregation. I watched as a girl named Anna made a beeline toward me. She handed me her flower with a look of love that was indescribable.

Later in the service, as I listened to the sermon, the pastor made reference several times to mothers who had lost a child. Afterwards, the minister told me that he had me in mind when he wrote his message.

After church, I had lunch with my other son, and we had a truly wonderful afternoon and evening. I felt God's profound love, and I realised that he had been caring for me all along by sending people to love and support me.

My life has been permanently changed by my son's death. But I now know firsthand that no matter where life takes me, God loves me, cares for me and is always there for me.

Prayer: *Dear God, thank you for always being there for us and for letting us know the power of your love in all things. Amen*

Thought for the day: Especially during my darkest hours, God shines a light of love and peace.

Jenny Donaldson (Missouri, US)

Small things

Read John 21:4–12
Even the very hairs of your head are all numbered.
Matthew 10:30 (NIV)

My friend Andrew told me that he prays only when he has problems that he cannot solve on his own. In contrast, I often call on the Lord for help with small things: 'Lord, help me find a place to park my car' or 'What souvenirs shall I buy for this friend, Lord?' or 'Lord, where have I placed my car keys?' After seeing me praying often about trivial things in daily life, Andrew bluntly said, 'I don't want to bother God with small things.'

Today's reading tells us that Jesus cared when the disciples caught nothing after a whole night at sea. Today's quoted verse reminds us that God also cares about the minor details of our lives. After all, he knows how many hairs are on our heads! God listens to my friend's prayers about big problems and also to my prayers about the little things that bother me in daily life. Nothing is too insignificant for God, who cares about the big and small things that happen to us. We can go to him with anything because he loves us.

Prayer: *Dear God, you care about what happens in our lives. Help us to come to you with all the concerns in our lives. Amen*

Thought for the day: God wants to hear all my concerns – big and small.

Timothy Tay (Sarawak, Malaysia)

All-surpassing power

Read 2 Corinthians 4:7–15

We have this treasure in jars of clay to show that this all-surpassing power is from God and not from us.

2 Corinthians 4:7 (NIV)

I had lived my whole life with my hands jerking out of my control. I thought it was normal. It wasn't until high school that I learned how serious my condition was. One Sunday morning, I had a grand-mal seizure. One moment I was in the kitchen and the next in an ambulance. I was diagnosed with epilepsy, chronic migraines, and a heart condition that made me susceptible to dizziness. During my first year at high school, I used a wheelchair because I was too unstable to walk. I felt limited by my health and judged by my peers; but I also kept remembering that no matter how weak I am, God is strong.

As believers, we have the all-surpassing power of God inside us. Although my body was unpredictable and weak, I was being upheld by God. When I became scared or my body tightened as if about to seize, I would call out to him and he would answer. Through all of the seemingly endless doctor's appointments and emergency hospital visits God never left me.

I find comfort in knowing that God lives in me and will never leave me. Despite my diagnosis, I can face each day with renewed faith, knowing that my soul is well and that nothing of this world can crush or destroy me because God is with me.

Prayer: *Dear Lord, use us for your purpose and to bring glory to your name. Amen*

Thought for the day: Because God is with me, I can face anything today brings.

Lindsay West (Texas, US)

Violets

Read Galatians 5:22–26

Let us throw off everything that hinders and the sin that so easily entangles.
Hebrews 12:1 (NIV)

I have a garden full of violets. They look lovely in the spring, when everything is covered with a faint purple haze. The problem is, I have a garden very full of violets. They smother everything. I also have a very heavy clay soil and it makes getting the violets out very hard work. Because, although I love violets, I also need other things in the garden if it is to look balanced.

Every time I try to weed or thin them out I am reminded of the verse from Hebrews above. If I am to grow spiritually I need a balance of all the fruit of the Spirit, just as my garden needs a balance of different flowers if it is to be healthy.

Although the violets grow back again it's not so difficult to get them out next time because the roots are not so deep. I trust that the same applies to my spiritual life – every time I 'weed out' some sin, although it tries to creep back, it's not so difficult to remove it from my life another time, because by the grace of God I am growing towards him. Every time I feed my mind on the 'whatsoever things' (Philippians 4:8), I am making it harder for sin to grow in me.

Prayer: *Dear Lord, help me always to grow in the knowledge and love of Christ. Amen*

Thought for the day: What 'weeds' do I need to remove from my life today?

Hilary Hartley (Sussex, England)

A new dream

Read Isaiah 43:14–21

The Lord says, 'Behold, I will do a new thing.'
Isaiah 43:19 (KJV)

The job opportunity of my dreams had practically fallen into my lap. It would be a way to use my talents and to earn an income. But trouble arose from the start, and it did not work out as I had hoped; the door closed in my face. I was hurt and disappointed and found myself unable to let go. I wanted to pry the door back open and make this job work. After all, this was my dream!

We often find ourselves at such a crossroads – a lost job, the end of a marriage, the death of a loved one – and all our dreams seem to go up in smoke. We stand looking back at the rubble and long for what might have been.

During this difficult time, God gently reminded me of Isaiah 43. The Israelites needed to forget what lay behind. God was doing something new for them, and he wanted to do something new for me. I just had to stop looking back. As I let these words from Isaiah soak into my mind and heart, I was able to take a step forward. Before I knew it, other job opportunities opened up and I began to get excited once more. God was giving me new dreams. I just had to turn and face the right direction – toward him.

Prayer: *Dear Lord, thank you for never leaving us stuck in the past. Give us new dreams and new beginnings. Amen*

Thought for the day: When I turn toward God, I can find a new beginning.

Belle Todd (Texas, US)

Spiritual inheritance

Read Malachi 3:7–12

Peter said, 'Silver or gold I do not have, but what I do have I give you. In the name of Jesus Christ of Nazareth, walk.'
Acts 3:6 (NIV)

My parents raised five of us on a meagre income. My dad had a very basic education and mother was completely illiterate. At a time when none of the Christian families in our area owned a Bible, my dad purchased a Bible for me before I was born. One day when I was eleven, my dad told me about the Bible and shared part of today's reading, 'Test me in this,' says the Lord Almighty, 'and see if I will not throw open the floodgates of heaven and pour out so much blessing that there will not be room enough to store it' (Malachi 3:10, NIV).

Hearing my dad read this scripture moved me deeply, and I committed myself to the Lord. I did not inherit gold or silver from my parents, but they gave me a great love for God and for scripture. The blessings I have enjoyed throughout my life are the result of this spiritual inheritance. Now, as a father and grandfather, the goal of my life is to do the same for my children and grandchildren. I teach them that if we have the whole world at our disposal but do not have the Lord, we have nothing. On the other hand, if we have nothing but the Lord, we are richer than we would be if we had the whole world.

Prayer: *Dear Father, thank you for the godly inheritance we have received. Help us to share your love with future generations. Amen*

Thought for the day: The best inheritance I can leave for younger generations is an example of a godly life.

Ishwarbhai Hirabhai Dabhi (Gujarat, India)

Endurance

Read Exodus 13:3–5

O give thanks to the Lord, for he is good, for his steadfast love endures for ever.
Psalm 136:1 (NRSV)

One July day at a garden centre near my home, I noticed some bedraggled rose plants with no blooms and browning leaves on sale for half price. Unable to resist a bargain, I bought two and planted them under a tree. Each week I watered them but saw little improvement. When winter brought snow and ice, I feared they would not survive.

Months passed, and on a rainy morning I was preparing a Bible study about the Israelites' escape from Egypt. As I pondered their wilderness hardships, my dog began barking at the back door. I opened it, and she leapt past me to chase a squirrel up the tree. I hurried to the tree to get her out of the rain. Nestled among the dead leaves on the ground, something green caught my eye. The unpromising roses had endured winter's harsh weather and had started to put out new growth.

The plants' endurance brought me back to the Exodus story. The Israelites experienced many hardships during their journey, but God's grace, love and forgiveness supported them through bitter days, and they survived to thrive in a new land. Like the Israelites, we experience difficult times. My roses remind me that endurance and survival are not always easy, but that the God who travelled with the Israelites also travels with us.

Prayer: *Gracious God, help us remember that during difficult times you are still walking beside us. Amen*

Thought for the day: God does not expect me to face hardships alone.

Jewel Deane Suddath (North Carolina, US)

Prayer works

Read Ephesians 6:18–19

I can do all things through Christ which strengtheneth me.
Philippians 4:13 (KJV)

Recently a routine eye exam revealed a macular hole in my left eye. I had not noticed any changes in my vision, but I was suddenly in danger of losing my sight and needed surgery immediately.

Anxiety overwhelmed me. I tried to cope on my own by reading scripture and reciting memorised verses, including today's verse. I reached out to my minister to ask for prayers for my doctors, my husband and me. I began to feel some relief. I was hesitant to seek help on social media, but what better way to ask for prayers from many friends?

As I was getting ready the night before surgery, I was surrounded by calm feelings of peace, warmth and safety. My anxiety left me. I felt the prayers working in my life in a way I had never felt before. Reading the thoughts and prayers of my social media friends helped me face my health issue. Reaching out to others who share my faith in God gave me strength. I know prayer works, so I continue to pray for others no matter how the request comes.

Prayer: *Dear God, thank you for the strength Christ brings us when we pray. Amen*

Thought for the day: My prayers can strengthen others.

Mary Ellen Piland (North Carolina, US)

PRAYER FOCUS: SOMEONE ANTICIPATING EYE SURGERY

Open your eyes!

Read Psalm 40:4–8
Taste and see that the Lord is good.
Psalm 34:8 (NIV)

In the past year we have planted a large courtyard garden of cherry trees, white roses and a box hedge. In the autumn my husband put in about 90 daffodil bulbs among the other plants. Every day since I have enjoyed looking at our garden. Recently I realised, to my surprise, that some of the daffodil shoots were poking up above the soil – a few were quite tall already. I hadn't expected to see them so soon, so I hadn't noticed them before.

We often miss God's blessings in our lives simply because we fail to notice them. In times of difficulty, busyness or stress we may focus on the tasks we must complete or the problems we must tackle and fail to see the good things that are around us all the time – the beauty of trees and flowers, the kind words of supportive friends, the smile of a loving grandchild, the friendliness of strangers. If we take a moment to open our eyes and hearts, we can give thanks for the blessings that remind us that God loves us and cares for us – even when trying circumstances cause us to forget. Thanks be to God!

Prayer: *Loving God, thank you for your love which surrounds us every day of our lives. Remind us that you care for us, and open our eyes to see the blessings you give us. Amen*

Thought for the day: Whenever I look for God's blessings, I always find them.

Margaret Martin (Australian Capital Territory, Australia)

Sacred bonds of love

Read Revelation 21:1–7

Blessed are those who mourn, for they will be comforted.
Matthew 5:4 (NRSV)

I have mourned the death of my parents, a young niece and many others; but nothing has been as difficult as the death of my husband. It has been four years since he died, and still I have days that are simply hard to get through. As Christians, both my husband and I knew where he was going, and I am certain that someday I will join him there. But the time in between is sometimes overwhelming.

Jesus said, 'Blessed are those who mourn, for they will be comforted.' Because of my faith, I sense the comfort and presence of Jesus every day. That doesn't mean that some days I don't miss my husband beyond words, but it does mean that I acknowledge that 'the Lord gave, and the Lord hath taken away; blessed be the name of the Lord' (Job 1:21, KJV).

We each have a life journey, and our time here is limited. We form many sacred bonds with people, and God calls us to cherish these bonds and to love those whom he gives to us. When we do, we find the comfort that comes only through the peace that passes all understanding – found in Christ Jesus, our Lord and Saviour.

Prayer: *God of love and mercy, help those who mourn, and grant them comfort through faith in Christ, our Lord. In Jesus' name. Amen*

Thought for the day: I can take comfort in the peace of Jesus Christ.

Mary A. Potter (North Carolina, US)

My mission

Read Acts 20:20–24

Nothing, not even my life, is more important than my completing my mission... to testify about the good news of God's grace.
Acts 20:24 (CEB)

For many years I have wondered, 'What is my mission in life?' I am a retired police detective. My career was cut short because of a stroke that left me with a speech impediment and the need to use a walker for balance. I thought that my life's mission was over.

But then I remembered a tape a friend had given me. I listened to its spiritual and inspirational message again and remembered that the speaker also has a speech impediment. Even with a speech impairment greater than mine, this speaker talks to hundreds of people each year, telling them the good news of Jesus!

Because of this speaker and today's quoted verse, I have rediscovered the mission for my life – to spread the good news of Jesus. I now give inspirational, spiritual and motivational presentations to other stroke survivors in hospitals and churches. My public speaking gives me the opportunity to spread the good news of Jesus. Even with my speech impediment and my walker, I have found that I can complete my mission in life – the mission God has given me.

Prayer: *Dear Lord, help us to embrace and fulfil the mission you have given each of us. Amen*

Thought for the day: No matter what my abilities are, God has a mission for me.

Ron Sanders (Michigan, US)

Do not judge others

Read John 8:1–11

Do not judge, or you too will be judged. For in the same way as you judge others, you will be judged, and with the measure you use, it will be measured to you.

Matthew 7:1–2 (NIV)

As I arrived at church one Sunday, I congratulated myself for being on time for the service and for praying for those I saw walking or running instead of preparing to attend worship. But I found only one other car in the car park. Where was everybody? Had I missed an announcement? I had been feeling out of the loop since moving to a retirement community. I took out my mobile phone and called another church member. 'Where is everyone?' I asked.

'It's Saturday,' she replied.

'Oh, so it is! The joke's on me!' I laughed.

Then I began to reflect on the morning. When I left my flat, I had thought critically of the two workmen repairing a door for my neighbour. As I approached the church, I saw a man mowing his lawn. 'On Sunday!' I thought, shaking my head.

That day reminded me of the danger of jumping to conclusions. When we rush to judge, we can hurt other people. I reminded myself to be slower to judge others.

Prayer: *Dear Father, guard our minds and our lives that we may not judge others. Help us to be a blessing to those around us. In Jesus' name. Amen*

Thought for the day: Today I will treat others the way I want to be treated (see Luke 6:31).

Sybil Austin Skakle (North Carolina, US)

The rescue

Read Genesis 1:20–25

We are God's handiwork, created in Christ Jesus to do good works, which God prepared in advance for us to do.
Ephesians 2:10 (NIV)

One sunny day my sister and I went to a craft fair to sell our hand-painted gourds. We took turns looking after the stall and alternated lunch breaks. When I returned from lunch, my sister told me about a stray dog she had seen gasping for breath. Later, she saw the dog again when it was her turn to go to lunch. She fed the dog and gave him a drink of water, and when it was time for her to return to the stall, she asked a staff member at the fair to look after him.

Later in the evening, the dog was still in the care of the volunteer but was quite happy to see us. Our mum allowed the dog to stay overnight with us so that we could take him to the vet the next day. The vet told us that the dog was suffering from malnutrition and neglect. In that condition, he said, the dog would not have lived much longer.

That day, the meditation in *El Aposento Alto* (the Spanish edition of *The Upper Room*) was about missed opportunities to help others in need. The meditation resonated with me as I thought about our encounter with this dog. Though the meditation was about helping people, I know that God cares for all of creation and for all creatures. And I was sure that God wanted us to help this dog. Since that day, the dog, whom we named Pedro, has been a member of our family.

Prayer: *Creator God, thank you for being the beacon for all humankind. May we always be prepared to care for those in difficult and vulnerable situations. Amen*

Thought for the day: What shall I do to care for God's creation today?

Sandra Perdomo (Cali, Colombia)

Rest for the weary

Read Matthew 11:25–30

Jesus said, 'Come to me, all you who are struggling hard and carrying heavy loads, and I will give you rest.'
Matthew 11:28 (CEB)

As I was picking blueberries one July morning, I watched the heavily laden branches of fruit spring up little by little as the plump, juicy berries were removed. 'Ahhh!' the bush seemed to say when its branches no longer hung down to the ground, putting stress on the woody stems. Seeing how the shrubs bowed beneath their substantial loads of berries made me think of Jesus' promise in today's verse.

Obviously blueberry bushes don't suffer from the same type of burdens that humans do. But like blueberry bushes, we can become weak and non-productive as we are weighed down by burdens. When we try to cope with problems all by ourselves, our health and lives are affected by worry, fear, anger, sadness and other destructive emotions. The burdens that weigh us down might be unmanageable workloads, financial worries, marital problems, family issues, illness, alcohol, drugs or even problems within our church family. Like the blueberry bush, we need help in shedding our load. When we are weary, we can trust in Jesus, who promises to give us rest.

Prayer: *Heavenly Father, thank you for relieving us of our burdens. In Christ's holy name we pray. Amen*

Thought for the day: Jesus will give me rest when I give my burdens to him.

Lara Beard (Kentucky, US)

View from the top

Read Psalm 27:1–6

[God] shall set me up upon a rock. And now shall mine head be lifted up above mine enemies round about me.
Psalm 27:5–6 (KJV)

As morning dawned over the hills, my wife and I began our hike to Ramona Falls in the Mount Hood Wilderness area of Oregon. Halfway to the falls, we broke through a dense forest and came upon a towering rock formation, previously hidden from view. From atop the cliff, we could see for miles around.

In today's Bible reading, David wanted God to hide him from his enemies. Ironically, God set him high upon a rock, which left David in plain sight of these adversaries. Whether a physical location or a spiritual experience, this higher vantage point gave David a new perspective. His enemies looked feeble and his problems small when compared to the greatness of God.

Christians have adversaries too. Trials and temptations may test our faith, causing fear and doubt. At times these battles are severe, and we may feel like hiding. But Christ wants us to see these enemies for what they really are: defeated foes. We know that we can trust God to lead us to victory.

Prayer: *Mighty God, thank you for being the rock of our salvation. Help us to put our trust in you. Amen*

Thought for the day: In Christ, our battles are already won.

Charles Earl Harrel (Oregon, US)

Above and beyond

Read Hebrews 6:9–12

Keep control of yourself in all circumstances. Endure suffering, do the work of a preacher of the good news, and carry out your service fully.
2 Timothy 4:5 (CEB)

Every Sunday our church sends a team of people to a local park with a hot meal to share with those who are hungry. Although I am part of that team, I am often tired and grumpy about serving food in the park on a Sunday afternoon. I would rather go home and have a nap or enjoy a walk on the beach by myself. But when I hear a hungry mother say thank you for a plate of food or when I share a friendly conversation with a stranger over the meal, I forget about how much I wanted that nap or walk and remember that Jesus asks me to carry the message of God's love to others even when I am tired or unmotivated.

Being a servant of God means keeping this message alive. We are called to persevere in sharing with others the good news of Jesus. We are created to serve God. Since I call Jesus my Lord, I want to carry out this mission. I want to go above and beyond.

Prayer: *Dear Lord, fill us with zeal and joy to carry out your mission by serving others. We pray as Jesus taught us saying, 'Our Father in heaven, hallowed be your name, your kingdom come, your will be done, on earth as it is in heaven. Give us today our daily bread. Forgive us our debts, as we also have forgiven our debtors. And lead us not into temptation, but deliver us from the evil one.'* Amen*

Thought for the day: How will I go above and beyond in serving God this week?

Amy Swanson (California, US)

True sight

Read John 9:1–17
I was blind but now I see!
John 9:25 (NIV)

I sometimes think that if I could live my life again, I'd be an ophthalmic surgeon. What joy to be the means of enabling a physically blind person to see! I was unable to become a doctor; but I can help bring spiritual sight to the blind.

When asked to give my testimony, I find that the words of the blind man, miraculously healed by Jesus in the verse above, sum it up beautifully. Perhaps the greatest joy is to see the difference Christ makes in a person's life. Saul, after his experience on the road to Damascus, saw everything differently and was transformed. I have met many people whose lives have been transformed since encountering Jesus. One doctor, from a non-Christian family, has such zeal and love that in her spare time she goes with a team to Indian villages to provide free medical care and to share the love of Jesus. I know a former murderer who once carried a knife but now carries a Bible.

We were all lost and blind to spiritual realities until Jesus came to seek, find, rescue and share a personal relationship with us. Everything hinges on our response to him. When we realise who Jesus is and welcome him as Lord of our lives, we become like lights in the world.

Prayer: *Thank you, God, for opening our eyes to see who Jesus is and enabling us to help others to know your truth. Amen*

Thought for the day: Today I will be an example of Christ's love.

Lynda Samuel (Scotland)

Standing firm

Read Matthew 7:24–29

Jesus said, 'Everyone then who hears these words of mine and acts on them will be like a wise man who built his house on rock.'
Matthew 7:24 (NRSV)

Following years of declining health, my father's death was not unexpected, but it felt as if the earth had shifted under my feet. I felt as if I were no longer standing on firm, level ground.

The funeral took place in the church my father had attended all his life, the same church where he and my mother raised four children. When I entered that familiar building, I remembered how – decades before – my father had helped move massive amounts of earth, making the ground solid and level for an expansion of the church. This thought helped me to stand with renewed confidence that the physical ground beneath me was solid.

Then other memories from my childhood filled my mind – scenes of my father reading his Bible, praying, listening, asking questions, helping a neighbour in need. So many thoughts reminded me that my father built his life on a foundation of faith. Like the wise builder of the parable who builds his house on solid ground, we can put our trust in God. With such trust we can find comfort and assurance, allowing us to stand with confidence through the challenges of life.

Prayer: *Dear God, strengthen our faith. Help us trust in you and abide in your love even during times of struggle. Amen*

Thought for the day: What do my words and actions reveal about my faith in God?

Marti Williams-Martin (Tennessee, US)

Finding our way

Read Isaiah 55:8–11

In their hearts humans plan their course, but the Lord establishes their steps.
Proverbs 16:9 (NIV)

When I was young I wanted to join the Army. Later, I decided to become a college professor. Then, after starting a family, I decided to teach in a high school. But I couldn't get a job. I was frustrated because I loved teaching. Full of regret at the career I was giving up and thinking I was for ever closing the door to teaching, I became a police officer. Then I was given an opportunity to become a police training instructor. In this role I saw my education and passion come together.

Sometimes, when I look back at the path my life has taken, I feel as if I've been trying to find my way through a maze. At each turning, I guessed at what the final destination might be, but then my previous guess proved wrong. I haven't necessarily made wrong turns. My mistake was in thinking that I was in charge. Making plans was fine, but I have held too tightly to those plans rather than asking God for guidance.

As we try to find our way through life, making long-term plans is healthy and wise. But when we remember to hold our plans and choices loosely – submitting them to Christ and seeking godly counsel – we may discover that God has been working for our good all along.

Prayer: *Dear God, help us to seek your will and trust that you will guide us. Amen*

Thought for the day: What plans do I need to release to God today?

Stephen Johnson (California, US)

Under the broom tree

Sleep doesn't always come to me as easily as it once did. As I have grown older, I am sometimes wide awake until the small hours of the morning. For me, a sleepless night is usually accompanied by a good deal of anxiety. Concerns that don't bother me much in the daytime grow inordinately large by night. When these combine with my overactive imagination, I am done for.

As someone who has trouble sleeping, I am drawn to 1 Kings 19 where the prophet Elijah found rest and respite under a broom tree. At the beginning of chapter 19, Elijah was having a terrible time. Fearing for his life and fleeing to Horeb, he was all but ready to give up. Scripture says, '[Elijah] came to a broom tree, sat down under it and prayed that he might die. "I have had enough, Lord," he said. "Take my life; I am no better than my ancestors." Then he lay down under the tree and fell asleep' (vv. 4–5, NIV). I am amazed that, given Elijah's situation, he could fall asleep, just like that. Nothing on Elijah's mind was significant enough for him to lose sleep when he was in God's presence.

I love this moment in Elijah's story. At his wits' end and running for his life, he found rest in God's presence. I don't know how many nights I have wished sleep would come upon me so easily. Among the ways I occupy myself on sleepless nights is to eat biscuits and watch reruns of a popular television show from the 1980s. While not entirely productive, it distracts me from everything going on inside my head at two o'clock in the morning.

One sleepless night a few weeks ago, I decided to try something different. I started mentally going through the offices of the building I work in, praying for each of my colleagues. I named something about each person for which I am thankful, and then I asked God for something on his or her behalf – to watch over an ill family member, for help in a challenging work situation, for wisdom and guidance in making a big decision, for strength in caring for an ageing parent.

I have kept up this practice since. I haven't yet completed my walk through the entire building before falling asleep, so the next night I pick up where I left off. When I get to the last person in the last office, I start again. Some nights I neglect my prayers and go back to my biscuits and television for comfort instead. But more and more I use my sleepless nights to pray for my colleagues.

Elijah's story is only one of many that tell us just how much God cares for us. More than anything, the story is about the peace, trust, assurance and comfort that can come to us when we are in God's presence. It is a story about his care for those whom he loves. No matter what we are going through, what fears are swirling around inside our heads or what concerns weigh on us, we can go to God in prayer and find a little rest.

My midnight prayer practice has become for me a broom tree of sorts. It has brought me closer to God and given me a deeper sense of his care and protection for both myself and my colleagues, and ultimately given me rest. Above all, it has made me realise that the strength God gave Elijah is available to each of us as well, anytime and anywhere – under a solitary tree in the wilderness or in a living room chair.

Several meditations in this issue address God's continual care for us. You may want to read again the meditations for May 7, 25 and 29, June 9, 13 and 20, July 5, 8, 11, 22, 25, 29 and 30, and August 3, 5, 9, 11, 27 and 31 before responding to the reflection questions.

Questions for reflection

1 Name a story in scripture that has helped you in a significant way. What do you remember about the first time you encountered this story? Why is it meaningful for you?

2 What other characters in scripture did God care for in practical ways when they were enduring difficult situations? What do their stories teach us about how God cares for us when we go through tough times?

Andrew Garland Breeden
Associate Editor, Acquisitions

The wise builder

Read 1 Corinthians 3:1–15

I laid a foundation like a wise master builder... but someone else is building on top of it. Each person needs to pay attention to the way they build on it.
1 Corinthians 3:10 (CEB)

The experience of renovating a home while keeping up its normal operation can be stressful. Scheduling mealtimes, comings and goings, and discovering the need for unexpected repairs are just a few of the challenges we face. Only the thought of achieving our dream of having a new place that was designed just for us motivates us to continue.

The spiritual life is no different. Sometimes, our reforms are painful and difficult. But the certainty of transformation strengthens us in this process. The apostle Paul, in his first letter to the Corinthians, challenged them to a spiritual reform of their community. At the beginning of chapter 3, he warns about inappropriate behaviour, which showed spiritual immaturity, and he urged them toward spiritual maturity.

Just as we have the freedom to choose the materials and the best builder to renovate a house, we can choose how to build our spiritual lives. Guided by the word of God, we can either build our spiritual lives on the foundation of Christ, or we can choose to build with material wealth that has no eternal worth (1 Corinthians 3:12–13). It is up to us to choose wisely.

Prayer: *Dear God, strengthen and enable us to build and reform our lives so that they bring glory to you. In the name of Jesus. Amen*

Thought for the day: How will I build on the foundation Christ has laid?

Demetrio Henrique G. Soares (São Paulo, Brazil)

God's glorious colours

Read Psalm 145:9–13

All thy works shall praise thee, O Lord; and thy saints shall bless thee.
Psalm 145:10 (KJV)

As I was finishing the washing up the phone rang. It was my neighbour. I could tell from her voice that she was excited. 'Look out of your window,' she said. 'There's a beautiful double rainbow, and I didn't want you to miss it. It's just so bright and big!' I put the phone down, hurried to the back door, and there it was – a magnificent colourful arc stretching across the sky. I stood mesmerised by its grandeur.

Even if I live to be 110 years old, I will never tire of the beauty of nature. Whether it's a rainbow or an ocean, a lake, a river or a stream – nature captures my soul. I love the trees, the grass and the fields of flowers in the summertime. From regal rock formations to cascading waterfalls, from farmers' crops to city parks – they all draw me to their individual splendour. And as I drink it in, my final amazement is in the awesome God who created everything. Nature can remind us that the things that take our breath away were created by the One who gave us life and breath.

Prayer: *May we never forget that you, O God, are the creator of all the wonders of the world, especially us, your people. Amen*

Thought for the day: The power of God's creation can take my breath away!

Linda Fasking (Kentucky, US)

Out of my comfort zone

Read Isaiah 43:14–21

The Lord says, 'Forget the former things; do not dwell on the past. See, I am doing a new thing! Now it springs up; do you not perceive it? I am making a way in the wilderness and streams in the wasteland.'
Isaiah 43:18–19 (NIV)

Almost every summer I have had a holiday at a family property on a lake in Maine. I love to swim, but the lake temperature never warms up to the temperature of the air. As a child this didn't bother me; I could run in without caring or even feeling the coolness of the water. Now I find myself more cautious, slowly walking in one step at a time. I already know the water will be chilly, but I also know that it will feel good once I'm in. With only one foot in the cold water, however, I struggle to focus on the benefits of the swim.

As I reflected on this scenario, God showed me that I pull back from change in the same way when he leads me out of my comfort zone. Once it was starting a business from home so I that I could be there with my children. Another time it was taking online classes even though I had been out of education for many years. In both situations I had the goal in mind but hesitated to commit fully – just as I did when entering the cold lake.

To experience the abundant life God wants for me (John 10:10), I can't always stay in my comfort zone. Rather than facing change with fear, I want to press forward with perseverance, eager to follow God's next steps for my life.

Prayer: *Dear Lord, help us to follow you even when we feel uncomfortable or fearful. We want to trust you with our lives. Amen*

Thought for the day: Today I will embrace the changes God is placing before me.

Naomi Fata (New York, US)

Free sweetcorn

Read 2 Corinthians 9:6–8

[Remember] the words of the Lord Jesus… 'It is more blessed to give than to receive.'
Acts 20:35 (NRSV)

The farmers' market was loaded with vegetables at the height of the harvest. My wife and I moved through the crowd with our children, enjoying the sights and smells – and the samples! A farmer was standing in front of a truckload of sweetcorn and advertising with an appeal to neighbourliness: 'Buy a dozen ears and get an extra dozen free if you agree to do a favour for a neighbour.'

I watched people pass by. No one seemed interested – no one took the farmer's offer. I wondered if he actually would give us free corn for a verbal agreement. Perhaps that was the problem. Suppose there was a 'catch'? We approached the farmer and bought a dozen ears of corn. He asked if I wanted another dozen free for agreeing to do a favour for a neighbour. I said we would be glad to and then left.

For the past 30 years, that interaction in the farmers' market has played out in amazing ways. As I have given favours and generous quantities of garden vegetables to friends and neighbours alike, I have come to understand more deeply Paul's words in today's reading. That farmer inspired us to give freely, and in return we have not only got to know our neighbours but have also reaped the tremendous joy that comes from generosity.

Prayer: *Generous God, thank you for the privilege of sharing your abundant gifts with others. Though we cannot match your generosity, help us to develop a lifestyle of cheerful giving. Amen*

Thought for the day: For whom will I do a favour in God's name today?

Andy Freeman (North Carolina, US)

More than conquerors

Read Psalm 84:1–12

We are more than conquerors through him who loved us.
Romans 8:37 (NIV)

'It's too hard. I don't think I can do this,' said one of my students when I asked her to answer a maths question. Earlier she had started learning a new section of a maths lesson. As her tutor, I taught her how to remember the formula and to use it in problem-solving. I started testing her with easy questions and then moved to medium and hard ones. When she tried to solve the hard questions, I always encouraged her by saying, 'Don't worry. You can solve it. I'm here, ready to help you.'

This experience with my student reminded me how often I have been worried about the problems I have faced. Like her, I cried out, 'God, it's too hard for me! I cannot endure this.' At those times I forgot that Almighty God was always with me.

God is able to help us with our problems but not always by removing them. Instead, sometimes he teaches us and strengthens us to overcome our problems. He always stands by our side, showing us that we can be more than conquerors.

Prayer: *Thank you, God, for helping us to endure the challenges we face. We are not afraid because we know you are always with us. Amen*

Thought for the day: 'If God is for us, who can be against us?' (Romans 8:31).

Linawati Santoso (East Java, Indonesia)

'Focus!'

Read Matthew 6:25–34

Seek first [your heavenly Father's] kingdom and his righteousness, and all these things will be given to you as well.
Matthew 6:33 (NIV)

While I was sitting on the settee with my grandson, who had just finished his first term at college, my five-year-old granddaughter brought me a book so I could read her a bedtime story. For a few minutes, I continued to listen to my grandson's tales of college life. But growing impatient, my granddaughter finally said, 'Grandma! Focus!' We all had a good laugh, and then I read the story.

As I reflected on this the next day, I realised that listening to my grandson had been good, but at some point it was time for my focus to change to something else that was good. I wonder about the number of times that God might want to take hold of my arm and say, 'Ruth! Focus!' I am often busy with worthwhile activities – taking care of my family, teaching classes at church, and volunteering for other projects in the church and community. Sometimes I am so busy that I skip my devotions and quiet time with God. I approach my day with an agenda that leaves him out.

I believe that prioritising time with God is what Jesus meant when he said to seek first the kingdom. Each of us can ask, 'Is this where God wants me at this moment?' Putting our relationship with him first gives us the best possible perspective in life.

Prayer: *Dear God, help us to be quiet and to make time for you, so that we can put our focus where you want it to be. Amen*

Thought for the day: What is God asking me to focus on today?

Ruth Reazin (Kansas, US)

God, our strength

Read Psalm 18:1-6

[Jesus] said to his disciples, 'Why are you so afraid? Do you still have no faith?'
Mark 4:40 (NIV)

One day as I was travelling toward my native village, I was unable to see our small mountain, Pawagadh, due to the heavy fog. But I knew it was still there. In the same way, when we are in difficult situations and unable to see God's presence, he is still there, close to us.

When the doctor diagnosed my wife, Saroj, with cancer and said that she would live for only one or two more months, I was fearful at the thought of an uncertain future. However, this struggle and difficult situation brought me into a more intimate relationship with God.

Now, when I look back on this experience, I see that, even though Saroj has gone to be with the Lord, God was always with me during that time. He strengthened me and blessed my marriage and family life. We can call upon God's name, for he will always be with us.

Prayer: *Dear Lord, in all the difficult situations we experience in our lives, help us firmly to trust in you. Amen*

Thought for the day: In the storms of life, God is always present.

Ashok S. Rathod (Gujarat, India)

God is with us

Read Joshua 1:1–9

Be strong and courageous. Do not be afraid; do not be discouraged, for the Lord your God will be with you wherever you go.
Joshua 1:9 (NIV)

My husband and I were praying about moving our family across the country to help launch a new ministry. Leaving family, friends and a good job behind made the decision hard, but we felt that God was urging us to go. One night when my heart felt heavy about leaving, I was reading the scripture passage above from Joshua. As I read that God asked Joshua to move not only his family but an entire nation into a new land, the words almost leapt off the page at me. Instantly, I felt God's peace fill me. I knew that he was asking us to go and promising to be with us.

After we had put the children to bed, I shared this insight with my husband. He jumped up to get a scrap of paper from his shirt pocket that one of his students had given him. On it, the student had written the exact same verse. We thanked God for reassuring us in such an amazing way.

When God asks us to do something new or challenging, he will be with us – giving us the strength and courage to obey. Every time we read scripture and ask him to help us apply it to our lives, we can watch and wait. God is faithful to encourage us along the way.

Prayer: *Thank you, God, for giving us the strength and courage to do what you have called us to do. Amen*

Thought for the day: Today I will read scripture and listen for God's leading.

Sara Hague (Oregon, US)

Rock-solid faith

Read Hebrews 11:1–10

Trust in the Lord for ever, for the Lord, the Lord himself, is the Rock eternal.
Isaiah 26:4 (NIV)

I have recently been inspired and encouraged by the rock-solid faith displayed by two of my friends in very difficult circumstances. Muriel, who is in her eighties, lost her friend of 64 years to cancer. She wrote to tell me with absolute certainty that Betty had 'gone to glory early this morning'.

Susan's 27-year-old daughter, Felicity, received treatment for breast cancer last year but has now been diagnosed with a liver tumour and needs more chemotherapy. Despite her heartache and grief, Susan told me unwaveringly that her daughter's future was in God's hands.

In Luke 6:46–49, Jesus tells the story of the wise man who built his house on a foundation of rock. Because of this firm foundation, the house was able to withstand any catastrophe that the weather could throw at it. Jesus commends people, like my friends Muriel and Susan, whose faith in God is unswerving no matter how hard their circumstances are. It is one thing to have faith when everything is going well; but when troubles assail us, we need the comforting strength of God's presence with us to help us cope and survive.

What a blessing it is to have friends of strong faith whose powerful witness is an encouragement to all who know them!

Prayer: *Dear God, deepen our faith so that we may learn to rely on your love and strength in every situation. Amen*

Thought for the day: God is the only sure foundation for life.

Margaret Martin (Australian Capital Territory, Australia)

PRAYER FOCUS: SOMEONE WHO HAS LOST A CLOSE FRIEND

The Livermore light bulb

Read Matthew 5:14–16

God, who said, 'Let light shine out of darkness,' made his light shine in our hearts.
2 Corinthians 4:6 (NIV)

Fire station 6 in Livermore, California, draws visitors from all over the world. They come to see the world's most famous light bulb, a 60-watt bulb installed in 1901 which has been shining for over 115 years. That light bulb continues to baffle scientists who can't explain how it has managed to glow for so long. Physicists discovered that the bulb's filament, the heart of the bulb, is about eight times thicker than that of an ordinary bulb, giving it extraordinary durability. Also, since a bulb which is turned on and off will typically have a much shorter life span, the fact that this bulb shines 24 hours a day is part of the secret.

That light bulb in Livermore is a tangible reminder for me that if we consider the words of Jesus, we'll want to let others see the loving light of God constantly shining through us.

Like the filament in that bulb, God calls us to radiate light continuously, year after year. Jesus said, 'You are the light of the world', and 'Let your light shine before others, that they may see your good deeds and glorify your Father in heaven' (Matthew 5:14, 16). It is our privilege to glorify God and to share his light with others, so that they may glorify God as well.

Prayer: *Jesus, Light of the World, help us to share your light of love with those who pass through our lives. Amen*

Thought for the day: How will I glorify God today?

Steven Cohen (California, US)

Ebenezer

Read 1 Samuel 7:7–12

Samuel took a stone... and named it Ebenezer; for he said, 'Thus far the Lord has helped us.'
1 Samuel 7:12 (NRSV)

When I first sang the words, 'Here I raise mine Ebenezer; hither by thy help I'm come',* I had no idea what Ebenezer meant. Then I read today's scripture and learned that Ebenezer refers to a stone memorial that Samuel built to remind the people how much God had helped them. The word means 'Stone of Help'.

I recognise the Lord's daily help when I look back at my journals, which I now think of as 'Ebenezer journals'. Each day I make a list of ten things I am thankful for from the day before. I also make a list of prayer requests. The thank-you lists are often answers to the requests. Regardless of the year or date, as I flip open the pages I am always struck by God's faithfulness. I am especially thankful for these records on days when I question God's answers — or lack of answers.

When we remember God's help 'thus far', then, like Samuel, we can give thanks. And as we raise our Ebenezers, we need not doubt that help will come.

Prayer: *Loving Father, thank you for hearing our prayers. Help us to trust your faithfulness. Amen*

Thought for the day: What can I use as a reminder of God's faithfulness?

Deb Vellines (Missouri, US)

PRAYER FOCUS: THOSE STRUGGLING WITH DOUBT

*'Come, thou fount of every blessing', words by Robert Robinson, 1758.

Our intercessor

Read Romans 8:18–27
My help comes from the Lord, the Maker of heaven and earth.
Psalm 121:2 (NIV)

I usually begin each new year with a feeling of excitement at the chance for new beginnings. But the first month of 2014 did not hold much hope. My four-year-old son, Ben, was lying helpless in a hospital bed with a traumatic brain injury. For our family, a sense of sadness and hopelessness permeated everything. We didn't know what the future would hold or even if Ben would survive the next 24 hours.

I couldn't see past the bleakness of our current situation. Although I could feel that God was there in that dark place with us, I found that I couldn't manage more than a frantic prayer that I muttered over and over: 'God, please help us.' A short time later, I read Romans 8:27 – 'the Spirit intercedes for the saints' (NRSV).

The Spirit knows our innermost thoughts, our feelings and the desires of our hearts, and conveys them all to the Creator of the universe on our behalf. When we are at our weakest and don't have the words, the Spirit will intercede for us. The Spirit is always there, our constant helper. Even in the most helpless moments, that kind of love fills me with peace and hope.

Prayer: *Thank you, Lord, for the blessing of your Holy Spirit, who intercedes for us when we are at our weakest. Amen*

Thought for the day: When I don't have the words, the Spirit intercedes for me.

Karen Woodard (North Carolina, US)

Excess baggage

Read Hebrews 12:1–3

Let us throw off everything that hinders and the sin that so easily entangles. And let us run with perseverance the race marked out for us.
Hebrews 12:1 (NIV)

One day when I was looking for a particular pair of trousers, the wardrobe was so full I could not find them. Much to my surprise, I could not remember the last time I had worn half of the clothes in there. That day, they seemed to me like excess baggage. I decided then and there to clear out the wardrobe and donate many of the clothes. It is much tidier now.

My overflowing wardrobe resembles what sometimes happens in our lives. In our hearts we may store up envy, resentment, bitterness, and hurt – excess baggage that keeps us from becoming the people God wants us to be. Today is a good day to free our hearts from everything that does us harm and to seek a genuine relationship with God.

Prayer: *Almighty God, come and dwell in our hearts. Help us to release what is not pleasing in your sight so that we may find strength and gladness in you. We pray as Jesus taught us, saying, 'Our Father which art in heaven, Hallowed be thy name. Thy kingdom come. Thy will be done in earth, as it is in heaven. Give us this day our daily bread. And forgive us our debts, as we forgive our debtors. And lead us not into temptation, but deliver us from evil: For thine is the kingdom, and the power, and the glory, for ever. Amen'**

Thought for the day: 'Create in me a pure heart, O God' (Psalm 51:10).

Juan Julio Baez (Dominican Republic)

Listening to the river

Read John 16:32–33

The Lord said, 'If only you had paid attention to my commands, your peace would have been like a river.'
Isaiah 48:18 (NIV)

As I stood on the bank of smooth, white pebbles, the river surged past – morning sunlight glinting off the water. The river's steady roar filled me with peace. My husband and I had enjoyed a lovely weekend camping with families from our church, getting to know each other better, enjoying the river and praising God. Now we were taking one last walk before heading home. Each time a big truck rumbled past on the nearby road, the noise made me turn and look, disturbing my pensive mood. Then a thought dropped into my mind: 'Listen to the river.' Walking back to the car, I considered those words, and their meaning became clear. If I want to keep my peaceful feeling, I need to focus on the beauty of the river, not the distracting noises.

God's presence is like a river running through our lives. But life, like that road, is filled with distractions. Troubling news stories, illness and other personal struggles may bring worry; daily routines involving work, school and family require our attention. However, when we 'listen to the river' – by reading the Bible, meditating on its meaning and praying regularly – we can find God's peace, even in the midst of a busy life.

Prayer: *Dear God, thank you for the peace only you can give. Help us to focus beyond life's distractions to see you. Amen*

Thought for the day: How will I 'listen to the river' of God's peace today?

Susan Thogerson Maas (Oregon, US)

A friend who prays

Read Philippians 1:3–11

I thank God... as night and day I constantly remember you in my prayers.
2 Timothy 1:3 (NIV)

Every two weeks, another of our four young children came down with chickenpox. What's more, at the same time, my mother lay recovering in the hospital from her first cancer surgery. During each week, my husband was away, travelling for business. When I first went back to church after two months' absence, my dear friend greeted me with a huge hug. 'What's been happening?' she exclaimed. 'I've been praying and praying and praying for you!'

All that time, my friend had felt led to pray for me. I knew those prayers had helped our family endure this trying time. How precious is a friend who cares enough to pray for us without ceasing! This reminded me of Paul's words to Timothy, that he remembered him and prayed for him constantly.

We all know someone who needs prayer. It may be a friend battling disease or dealing with a wayward child or struggling after having lost their job. We can remember all those who are facing trials and pray that they will find the peace and strength to persevere.

Prayer: *Dear Lord, help us to love one another more and more, and remind us to pray for one another often. Amen*

Thought for the day: Today I will pray for a friend.

Mae Greenleaf (Florida, US)

Peace in a place of doubt

Read John 20:19–29

Jesus came and stood among them and said, 'Peace be with you.'
John 20:19 (NRSV)

At the end of the eight-mile hike to the top of Half-Dome in Yosemite National Park, we came face to face with the metal cables that would guide us to the top. Our whole group had hiked for hours, but when I finally saw the cables I refused to climb them, feeling it was dangerous and that I might fall 2,000 feet to my death. Watching my friends climb to the top, I started to feel embarrassed. Then, someone came behind me and said, 'I'll go with you.' Our group leader had pulled back from the group to make sure that I would not be left behind or fall off the cables. I slowly made it to the top, and we celebrated at the summit.

In today's reading – the account of Jesus' appearing to his disciples after the crucifixion – Thomas stubbornly refused to believe his friends' testimony that they had seen Jesus. In doing so, Thomas separated himself from the rest of the group. Then, without warning, Jesus appeared among them.

In times of doubt, it can feel as if God is absent. But, like our group leader who helped me get up the cables, God comes to us even at the height of doubt. When we are ready to turn back, he whispers, 'I'll go with you.'

Prayer: *Loving God, thank you for your persistent love that brings you alongside us even in our difficult and painful moments of doubt. Amen*

Thought for the day: Even in my times of deepest doubt, God is present.

Adam Benson (North Carolina, US)

Still serving others

Read Joshua 14:6–13

Let us not become weary in doing good, for at the proper time we will reap a harvest if we do not give up.
Galatians 6:9 (NIV)

A rose bush grows in a small memorial garden just outside our dining room window. The buds and early blossoms are a vivid yellow. Then, as the rose opens into full bloom, the petals become a gentle pink. Finally the colour of the rose changes again – this time to a pure white. Right up to the moment the petals fall, the rose radiates fragrance and beauty.

As I marvel at this wonder of nature, I am aware of the parallel with my own life. Young and vigorous, I poured my energies into active ministry. Then, in middle age, my vigour was directed into richer but quieter expressions. Now I approach my closing years and am marked by white hair and fading energy.

Yet, just as my rose radiates fragrance and beauty until the end, so, too, does my life. In my 82nd year, my physical drive and energy are limited. But God can still use my life to bless others through my prayers for those facing serious issues; my words of encouragement, guidance and support; my gifts of craftwork. Yes, I still have many ways in which I can bless others and serve God.

Prayer: *Dear Lord, enable us by your grace to love and serve one another. Amen*

Thought for the day: No matter how old I am, God can use my life to bless others.

Everard Blackman (Queensland, Australia)

Learning from Elijah

Read 1 Kings 19:1–14

Elijah said, 'The Israelites have forsaken your covenant, thrown down your altars, and killed your prophets with the sword. I alone am left, and they are seeking my life, to take it away.'
1 Kings 19:10 (NRSV)

I appreciate the prophet Elijah, not because he performed miracles or challenged false prophets but because he was so honest with God about his fears. In 1 Kings 18, Elijah challenged 450 prophets of Baal to see whose god would set fire to a sacrifice. Baal failed while God succeeded.

But Queen Jezebel told Elijah she would kill him in retaliation. Suddenly Elijah's courage vanished. He ran, hid and asked God to let him die. Instead, God sent food to strengthen him. But Elijah still complained. He went into a cave, and when God asked why he was there, Elijah repeated his complaint even after a personal display of God's power and presence. Showing divine patience, God told him to go and anoint others who would continue to cleanse the nation.

Elijah's honesty provides a window into how God responds to our complaints. He provided nourishment, strength, direction and help – without condemnation. Even in Elijah's doubt, God did not abandon him.

Elijah's story encourages me because it shows me that I'm not the only believer whose courage falters. And I can be honest with God even when my emotions aren't positive or reverent. Perhaps Elijah's weakest moments strengthen me the most.

Prayer: *Thank you, God, for reminding us that even in our weakness, you are willing and able to work through us. Amen*

Thought for the day: God already knows my weaknesses – and loves me anyway.

Jennifer Aaron (Washington, US)

Showing God's love

Read Psalm 34:1–10

I sought the Lord, and he answered me; he delivered me from all my fears.

Psalm 34:4 (NIV)

Recently, I went through three medical procedures for my prostate, bladder and colon. Initially I was worried because I had overheard the doctor say something about a round spot in one of my X-rays. However, friends reassured me with their prayers, and the results of the follow-up procedure turned out to be all clear.

When I shared some details of the procedures with my prayer group, one of them said that he was grateful to hear my story because he was preparing for a procedure himself. He was worried because he had no one to drive him home since his wife would be overseas that week and his only son was busy with school exams.

On that day, one of our group members turned up to stay with him at the hospital and drive him home. He was also given the all-clear by his doctor. From God, our friend had been given a double dose of peace: a clean bill of health and a friend to take him home.

Through our prayers and conversation, our prayer group has demonstrated God's love and care, reminding us that anyone can come forward to show God's love.

Prayer: *Dear Lord, thank you for giving us opportunities to show your love to our friends in need. Amen*

Thought for the day: How can I show God's powerful love to others today?

James Tang (Singapore)

Does it matter?

Read Hebrews 6:9–12

[God] will not forget your work and the love you have shown.
Hebrews 6:10 (NIV)

Driving through the summer-browned countryside of Romania, I heard one woman on my holiday Bible school team ask another, 'What is God teaching you this week?'

That question clanged around my mind for several days. What was God teaching me? Surely God had brought me to Romania to show me some life-altering truth. Yet among all the craft work and singing at meetings where most of the participants could not understand me, I couldn't see any lesson for me or any impact I may have had on them.

Until Wednesday. On Wednesday, a little girl handed me a daisy and a picture of rabbits and butterflies. Through a translator, her mother said, 'She comes to the Bible school because of you. She thinks you have a nice smile and that you sing pretty.' My heart melted, and in my heart God whispered, 'There's your lesson.'

When we go on mission trips, serve at soup kitchens or teach Sunday school for years on end, we might wonder if what we do matters. But that daisy and rabbit picture reminded me that when we obey God in the seemingly small work, he expands its impact in ways we could never imagine. Our call is to do the work.

Prayer: *Heavenly Father, help us take delight in doing the work you have given us to do, no matter how small it seems. May all we do bless others. Amen*

Thought for the day: No act of serving God is ever wasted.

Kristen G. Johnson (Washington, US)

An imperfect disciple

Read Luke 22:54–62

Peter followed at a distance.
Luke 22:54 (NIV)

We know that Peter was about to deny his Lord three times, in spite of his earlier protestations to the contrary. Yet he did have the courage to follow his Lord, albeit at a distance.

I know how easy it is to be a fair-weather friend of Jesus. I try to blend in when I'm with an unbelieving crowd, afraid to stand up for the truth of the gospel. I don't want to risk causing offence or feeling embarrassed. Yet when I have spoken up, it has usually been easier for me than I expected. The Lord promises us words to say (Luke 21:15), and our spirits are strengthened whenever we speak up for our faith.

It is heartening to know that Jesus knows our weaknesses and wants to love and restore us. Jesus foretold Peter's denials but also assured him that he had work for Peter to do in the future.

In the more than 50 years since I committed my life to Jesus, I have faltered and stumbled many times. But Jesus has been there to pick me up, just as he did with Peter in John 21:15–17. Even in our weakness, Jesus never gives up on us.

Prayer: *Dear Lord, forgive our hesitation to show our love for you. Strengthen us so that others may know you through us. Amen*

Thought for the day: How has Jesus strengthened me for the work he is calling me to?

Lynda Samuel (Scotland)

Providence

Read Genesis 50:15–26

Joseph said to his brothers, 'You intended to harm me, but God intended it for good to accomplish what is now being done, the saving of many lives.'
Genesis 50:20 (NIV)

The word providence speaks of God's divine care and guidance in our lives. This was certainly true in the life of Joseph whose brothers sorely mistreated him (see Genesis 37). But as Joseph reflected on all of his experiences in life, he could clearly see God's abiding care.

This sense of God's purpose was never more evident for me than when I accepted a position that would take my wife and me 8,000 miles from our home, our children and our grandchildren. It was a gut-wrenching decision. I prayed, fasted and sought the wisdom of others; through it all I trusted God for guidance. Though challenging, it turned out to be a most rewarding decision.

The older I become, the more I am able to see God's providence throughout my life. I often say, 'God's sovereignty is best seen in the rear-view mirror.' This does not cause me to be passive about life – just waiting for God to push me to the next event. Instead it creates in me a deep trust in my Creator who not only cares for me today but also directs my future, all for my good (see Romans 8:28). I continue to learn about God's providence daily. I hope that I am a good student.

Prayer: *Dear Lord, grant us your wisdom, strength, and courage as we seek your will and trust your guidance. Amen*

Thought for the day: In today's challenge, I will strive to see God's blessing for tomorrow.

Gary Miller (California, US)

A change of perspective

Read Psalm 27:4–8

We give thanks to you, O God... your name is near. People tell of your wondrous deeds.
Psalm 75:1 (NRSV)

We had a bumper crop of dandelions. My husband joked that if we killed them all, we wouldn't have anything left of our lawn. During this time, I was stuck gazing out my bedroom window at the lawn; I was in bed because I had a cancerous tumour. While I watched nature reclaim five years of hard work on our lawn, I wanted to cry. Then one day as I was looking out of the window, my four-year-old daughter, Gracie, nudged in beside me for a look. I heard her gasp. 'Oh, Mummy!' she said. 'Look at all the beautiful yellow flowers! Can we go and pick some?'

'Wow!' I thought. 'No wonder Jesus loves little children.' I had been so focused on the negative that I didn't see the beauty. I realised that I was only focusing on what I was missing out on because of my illness. Now I have begun to see that bed rest has given me more time for prayer and reading God's word than I've ever had before. How many times have I dismissed situations – or people – based on my negative perception of them?

We tend to see only what we look for. Psalm 19:1 says, 'The heavens declare the glory of God.' If I'm not seeing God's glory in all things, I need a change of perspective. Gracie made me determined to stop, no matter what circumstances surround me, no matter how things or people appear, and find the glory in all of God's creation.

Prayer: *Heavenly Father, help us to see in nature your glory and constant presence. Amen*

Thought for the day: Today I will look for God's glory in unexpected places.

Rebecca Olmstead (Washington, US)

Step out

Read John 15:12–16

Jesus said, 'You didn't choose me, but I chose you and appointed you so that you could go and produce fruit.'
John 15:16 (CEB)

Last summer I had the opportunity to go on a mission trip to New York City. As someone who struggles with claustrophobia and a fear of crowds, I wanted to avoid the chaos of big city streets and subways. I doubted that I would be able to make a difference. I made my decision not to go. God, however, had another plan. My friends gathered around me and encouraged me to go, and eventually I gave in, but I was still terrified.

One day, while we were working at a foodbank, a man arrived with a truck to be loaded with food for a delivery route. He handed me the keys, gave me the list of things he needed in the truck, and said he would be back in an hour. Nervously, I chose my team, and we set to work. When the man returned, his truck was loaded with everything he needed. Later, one of the youth leaders told me that the man had said that, thanks to our help, he was able to deliver food to more people than usual. I felt so proud that I had overcome my fear of New York City and was able to lead a team to get things done.

That trip was the best experience of my life. I learned that I could make a difference, despite being the least likely person for the job. When I trusted God enough to step out of my comfort zone, I realised that he had chosen me for the task and was with me every step of the way.

Prayer: *Dear God, help us to step beyond our routines to do your will so that we can shine your light to the world. Amen*

Thought for the day: Where is God encouraging me to go today?

Jo Hamilton (Pennsylvania, US)

Meaningful work

Read Psalm 37:23–31

A person's steps are made secure by the Lord when they delight in his way.
Psalm 37:23 (CEB)

After my graduation, I had difficulty finding a job. I went to a town in North Sumatra, but the job there did not work out; so I tried another town. I sent out application after application, searching for a decent job. I had hoped for an offer from one place in particular, but there was no answer from them.

One month earlier, the college I had graduated from had called me several times asking if I wanted to work there. I had not been eager to accept the offer because the salary was quite small. All this time, I had continued to pray to God to give me a decent job. But I had forgotten to listen for where the Lord was calling me to work. I forgot that longing for God means obeying when he sends me to a place where I can serve.

Now I am working to help the college's office staff. I firmly believe that the Lord provided a place and work for me, and that the place God chose is the best. Sometimes we imagine a wonderful and remarkable job, but the word of God says, 'Many are the plans in a person's heart, but it is the Lord's purpose that prevails' (Proverbs 19:21, NIV). When we listen for God's leading, he can use us to bless others so that we and they can experience his love in new ways.

Prayer: *Thank you, Lord, for showing us the way. Amen*

Thought for the day: I will let God lead me to meaningful ways to serve others.

Peter Hulu (Yogyakarta, Indonesia)

Don't be fooled

Read 1 Samuel 16:1–7

The Lord said to Samuel… 'People look at the outward appearance, but the Lord looks at the heart.'
1 Samuel 16:7 (NIV)

I put down the thin-skinned, brown-spotted orange and picked up a perfect, round navel orange. 'Don't be fooled by its looks,' a fellow shopper advised. 'The thin-skinned orange will be sweeter and juicier than the navel orange.' Largely to appease the other shopper, I took one of each. Yet, after I arrived home I was glad I took his advice. The orange I deemed as spotty and ugly was indeed the sweeter and juicier of the two.

How often have I been deceived by outward appearances, not only at the supermarket but at other times as well? How often have I been guilty of judging something or someone as less important – or less valuable or less worthy of my concern – by looks alone?

In John we hear Jesus saying, 'Do not judge by appearances, but judge with right judgement' (John 7:24, NRSV). That day this Bible verse took on a new, more practical meaning for me. I know for certain now that we cannot take anyone or anything at face value. Truly, it's what's inside that matters.

Prayer: *Dear God, help us remember to look beyond outward appearances and strive to view each of your creations through your eyes. Amen*

Thought for the day: Each person is God's beautiful creation.

Monica A. Andermann (New York, US)

God's word in my heart

Read Deuteronomy 11:18–21

Thy word have I hid in mine heart, that I might not sin against thee.
Psalm 119:11 (KJV)

Some time ago I was told that a neighbour had spoken negatively about me. I became furious and immediately went to confront, even to fight, that person. As I was dashing off, a Bible verse I had read came to my mind: 'Pursue peace with everyone, and the holiness without which no one will see the Lord' (Hebrews 12:14, NRSV). This stopped me in my tracks, and I turned back from what I wanted to do; I went back home immediately. I had decided to obey that word from God and not to fight. I had heard God's call to be at peace with everyone.

Reading, studying and memorising the word of God helps us to behave in ways that are pleasing to him. We can store up his word in our hearts and remember it before we take any action out of impatience or anger. Scripture will always help us not to fall short of God's expectations for our lives.

Prayer: *O Lord, help us to store up your word in our hearts so that we will not sin against you. We pray as Jesus taught us, saying, 'Father, hallowed be your name, your kingdom come. Give us each day our daily bread. Forgive us our sins, for we also forgive everyone who sins against us. And lead us not into temptation.'* Amen*

Thought for the day: Remembering God's word can keep me on the right path.

Fisayo Peters (Lagos, Nigeria)

PRAYER FOCUS: SOMEONE TEMPTED TO LASH OUT IN ANGER
*Luke 11:2–4, NIV

The gift of friendship

Read 1 Samuel 18:1–4

Some friends play at friendship but a true friend sticks closer than one's nearest kin.
Proverbs 18:24 (NRSV)

As eight-year-olds, a neighbour and I made a friendship pact and marked it with a special handshake and a wink. We promised to be there for each other and have fun together. Two years later, I was devastated when he and his family moved far away. As my grandmother consoled me, she encouraged me with words that still carry importance today: 'You have honoured your promise of friendship, and if your friend returns, I am sure you will remain friends.' This was my first lesson in covenant friendship.

I still grieve the loss of friends – whether due to distance or death – but I am grateful to God for whatever time I have with them. To me, friendship is a gift from God for our enjoyment as well as for our spiritual growth. God has a way of developing people to become relationally and spiritually committed friends who sharpen one another (Proverbs 27:17) and stick closer than family. This was evident with the friendship between Jonathan and David. God's way of bringing people into our lives and allowing us to become close friends is a precious gift indeed.

Prayer: *Heavenly Father, we praise you for the friendships you have given us. Help each of us to be a committed friend who shows the love of Christ to others. Amen*

Thought for the day: My friends are beautiful gifts from God.

Mike Medeiros (California, US)

Never lonely

Read John 14:15–19

Jesus said, 'I will not leave you comfortless: I will come to you.'
John 14:18 (KJV)

By the end of 2014, I found myself alone in our house nearly every day. My husband was working. Our daughter had married; our son had left for a job over 600 miles away. I began to miss the joy and intimacy of blessed family ties – all of us living together in our home of 32 years. It was difficult for me to adjust to these changed circumstances. Although there was endless household work to attend to and friendly neighbours and television to fill up my time, loneliness weighed heavily upon me. Every new day brought new worries.

However, I praise our living God for not leaving me alone. Every day he communicated with me as I read the Bible. God's promise given in Joshua 1:5 – 'I will never leave you nor forsake you' (NIV) – comforted and strengthened me. I placed my worries in his hands. I prayed for others. I grew in my faith as I learned to trust God more and more. This brought amazing peace into my heart.

My circumstances haven't changed, but my attitude has. I take comfort in Jesus' name. We have no friend like Jesus.

Prayer: *Thank you, Lord Jesus, for walking with us in our day-to-day lives and for assuring us that we can always come to you for help. Amen*

Thought for the day: My loneliness can be an opportunity to meet Jesus.

Ravina P. Diarsa (Gujarat, India)

I am not alone

Read Isaiah 43:1–3

The Lord said, 'You will call on me and come and pray to me, and I will listen to you. You will seek me and find me when you seek me with all your heart.'
Jeremiah 29:12–13 (NIV)

When I looked into the smiling, baby faces of my three sons and held their tiny fingers, I dreamed of all they'd grow up to be. Never did I imagine that decades later, one of my sons would struggle with drug addiction, and I would be visiting him in prison.

Devastated, I sobbed in the arms of family and friends. Doubtful, I joined a prayer group. Ashamed, I became involved with a support group for family and friends of addicts. Soon, I began to feel some comfort. Praying for one another, we were strengthened. A new understanding of addiction and its effects replaced my shame with compassion. With our hope renewed, our family became better together.

At times we may find ourselves trapped in a crisis and feeling helpless, alone, devastated or terrified. We may scream for help only to feel that no one hears or cares. But we are not alone. God loves us and doesn't want us to face our nightmares without help. He reaches out to show love for us through other people. Our scripture verse reminds us of the Lord's promise: 'You will seek me and find me when you seek me with all your heart.'

Prayer: *Thank you, compassionate God, for hearing our cries, listening to the prayers of our hearts, and helping us to find you in the love you show through others. In the name of your Son, Jesus Christ, we pray. Amen*

Thought for the day: God shows me love through the kindness and support of my friends.

Tammy Jones (Florida, US)

Compassionate Father

Read Psalm 103:1–14

As a father has compassion on his children, so the Lord has compassion on those who fear him.
Psalm 103:13 (NIV)

When I was seven, my dad bought me a bike and took me out to teach me how to ride it. At first, as I started, I would topple over and fall. So Dad would run along behind me – his hand on the seat – saying, 'Don't worry. I've got you. Keep pedalling.' Eventually he let go but kept chanting his words of assurance.

Even more than earthly fathers, God, our heavenly Father, cares for us. He knows that we are often like children learning a new task, trying our best but still toppling over. And our compassionate Father runs behind us, urging us along with, 'Keep going. I've got you.'

Jesus knew better than anyone the nature and qualities of his Father. He knew that God was with him always – from the desert where he was tempted by Satan to Gethsemane where he prayed that his suffering be relieved. Jesus showed us that our Father in heaven loves us and cares for us beyond anything we can imagine.

Prayer: *Heavenly Father, thank you for your great compassion that keeps us moving forward in faith. Amen*

Thought for the day: How can I show compassion toward God's children?

Tony Roberts (Indiana, US)

Focused thinking

Read Romans 11:33—12:2

Whatever is true, whatever is noble, whatever is right, whatever is pure, whatever is lovely, whatever is admirable – if anything is excellent or praiseworthy – think about such things.
Philippians 4:8 (NIV)

My husband is a mathematician. His education moulded his mind in ways that help him solve engineering problems. My own education in home economics formed my mind quite differently. The way we use our minds and the kinds of problems we solve shape the way we think.

The same can be true for Christians when we educate ourselves in scripture. Studying God's word shapes our minds and changes the way we think. In today's quoted verse, Paul even goes so far as to tell us what to think about. Contemplating this verse, I realised that what Paul asks us to think about is a list of God's character traits. God is truth and righteousness. He is pure and noble. When we think about who God is and what he is like, our minds can be transformed. Perhaps this is what the Bible means when it tells us to fix our thoughts on Jesus (see Hebrews 3:1).

Many writers throughout the ages have urged Christians to study the Bible and memorise scripture. How exciting and astonishing that doing this can actually change the way we think, renewing and transforming our minds (see Romans 12:2). What wonderful news! Memorising Philippians 4:8 is a great place for us to start.

Prayer: *Blessed Lord, we praise you for your written word that has the power to change us through the renewing of our minds. Amen*

Thought for the day: If I focus my mind on godly thoughts, I can be more conformed to the image of Christ.

Jane Reid (Oregon, US)

Can't stop praising

Read Psalm 145:1–12

Through [Jesus]... let us continually offer a sacrifice of praise to God, that is, the fruit of lips that confess his name.
Hebrews 13:15 (NRSV)

We can easily tell when someone is in love. This person is full of life and can't stop talking about his or her significant other. I could see this when my niece interviewed a couple for a school appointment. When they were asked to describe each other, Mary said of her husband, Eric: 'I am blessed to have him.' 'She's a great woman,' Eric responded. 'No, you're the best,' Mary replied. Neither wanted to be the one to stop first.

Similarly, those who love the Lord are full of life and hope, knowing that the love they've found surpasses any relationship that the world can offer. Because of this, they can't stop praising God.

All relationships, even our relationship with the Lord, go through challenges. Can we still praise God when our prayers seemingly go unanswered or when plans that seemed like God's will don't turn out the way we expect?

The last question my niece asked the couple was: 'How has your relationship lasted all these 30 years?' Both agreed that communication sustains a relationship. Regular prayer and acts of devotion – even when we don't feel like it – sustain our relationship with God. These, along with reading the Bible, teach us how to praise him in every situation.

Prayer: *Loving Father, help us love you the way you want to be loved so we can praise you the way you deserve to be praised. Amen*

Thought for the day: My love for God inspires continual praise.

Juvelyn Lumberio (Cavite, Philippines)

When the brook dries up

Read 1 Kings 17:1–9

It came to pass after a while, that the brook dried up, because there had been no rain in the land. And the word of the Lord came unto [Elijah].
1 Kings 17:7–8 (KJV)

One Wednesday morning, my boss beckoned me into his office. Instead of receiving the usual briefing for my work, I received a small severance package, terminating my position. Driving home and holding back tears, I thought about my four-month-old son whose traumatic birth had required heart surgery. The hospital visits and bills for an oxygen tank weighed on my shoulders. How could I care for my son's needs with no income?

Often we do not understand why we face trials like these. But God's own prophet Elijah endured a drought for three years, living only on bread from ravens and water from a brook. After all hope had vanished, Elijah learned to trust in God's care and timing. Elijah's rescue came only after the brook had dried up.

God knows our needs even better than we do. Sometimes we don't receive the specific help we think we need. But, like the apostle Paul, who prayed fervently for healing, we can learn to glory in our sufferings so that God's strength will be manifest (see 2 Corinthians 12:9). At other times the answer is better than we could hope for. One week after losing my job, God provided me with a better one. Now my son is happy, healthy, and growing. Our faith can flourish when we trust in God's timing.

Prayer: *Dear God, help us to trust your wisdom in times of drought when the brook dries up so that we build our faith in you and not in ourselves. Amen*

Thought for the day: When the brook dries up, I can rely on God to provide.

Daniel Mynyk (Colorado, US)

New life

Read Isaiah 11:1–10

A shoot will come up from the stump of Jesse; from his roots a Branch will bear fruit.
Isaiah 11:1 (NIV)

Within a month, our community had been affected by two hurricanes. The first, Hurricane Hermine, had hit us directly – leaving in its wake fallen trees, power cuts and broken lives. A month later, the second storm, Hurricane Matthew, barely grazed us, but its path of destruction only heightened our sense of anxiety as we watched the devastation from afar. During this time, I was struggling with my own storms and the brokenness of family problems.

Still on edge, after the second storm, I walked by a neighbour's tree, which had been cut nearly in half by Hurricane Hermine. Since then, the broken branches had been removed and the deep cut in the tree had been sealed. When I looked closer, I noticed new leaves breaking out of the cut. Amazed, I examined it more closely and saw a fresh new limb forming out of the dead-looking part of the tree.

This immediately lifted my spirits and brought deep hope into my day and my life. I thought of the passage about new life forming from the broken, dead stump of Jesse and the way in which that new root ultimately brought the hope of Jesus. Whether brought on by nature or human frailty and sin, whenever the storms of life threaten to over-whelm us, God's deep grace and peace will intercede.

Prayer: *Thank you, God, for reminding us that you are with us in all the storms of life. Amen*

Thought for the day: God can take something broken in my life and make it new.

Patricia M. Daniels (Florida, US)

Back on our feet

Read Mark 4:35–41
Jesus said, 'Peace! Be still!'
Mark 4:39 (NRSV)

My family and I had finally escaped homelessness and were fighting to start again. We had nothing – no furniture for the small flat we rented, not even beds. We sat and slept on the floor. We had no dishes or pans for cooking. Everything we once owned had been sold long before to try to avoid becoming homeless. Now we struggled to find jobs and buy food. I was fearful that we would fail and be back to living in a car. I was overwhelmed, and the more I focused on my problems, the bigger they seemed.

One day, as I was washing my children's clothes in the bath, feeling I had lost my way and lost my peace, I stopped and prayed for God's help. After hanging the clothes to dry on the fence outside, I went up to my room, sat on the floor, and started to read my Bible. When I came to Mark 4, where Jesus calmed a storm with the words 'Peace! Be still!' I said the words over and over, 'Peace! Be still!' I realised that the problems I faced were not bigger than God.

I held on strongly to the peace of God, and in time we got back on our feet. Our trust in God grants us the peace we need to face life's problems.

Prayer: *Loving God, grant us the peace that only you can give us. Amen*

Thought for the day: I have the peace of God that passes all understanding (see Philippians 4:7).

Judy Ann Eichstedt (Oklahoma, US)

Working for our good

Read Romans 8:28–39

We know that all things work together for good for those who love God, who are called according to his purpose.
Romans 8:28 (NRSV)

In 2016, my brother took a college entrance examination. On the day of the examination the computer system failed, which led to his losing some already-answered questions and prevented him from completing many others. When the test results were released, he didn't score well enough to be admitted to the college. We felt discouraged and questioned God's promises.

In spite of the situation, we still gathered at night to study God's word. Reading God's message to us in Romans 8:28 strengthened our hearts. A week later, we received news that the education staff had reconsidered the results. They added 40 points to the scores of those who experienced technical problems during the examination, including my brother. We praised God for such a blessing.

We are often pressured by events that shake our faith and our trust in God. But we can be encouraged, knowing that all things work for our good – not because of our qualifications but because of God's love and faithfulness. When we remain faithful and continue to trust in God, we can find the hope and courage to persevere.

Prayer: *Dear Lord, help us to trust you in the midst of life's challenges, knowing that you are working for our good. In the name of Jesus. Amen*

Thought for the day: When technology fails, Jesus doesn't.

Esther Nwogwugwu (Rivers State, Nigeria)

Jesus is our guide

Read Psalm 25:4–10

I will instruct you and teach you the way you should go.
Psalm 32:8 (NRSV)

We arrived for a weekend with my older son at his college. He led us through the car park to the entrance of a hiking trail. 'Have you ever been on this trail before?' I asked. 'No. But we'll just follow it and see where it leads,' my son replied confidently. 'OK,' I thought as we began, but I wondered where we would find ourselves at the end of the trail. It was slightly overgrown in places, and all we could rely on was the path in front of us. We followed the path, trusting that it would lead us through. It did! We passed some beautiful scenery and animals along the way, and finally reached the end, happy and safe.

Sometimes our lives can be like following an overgrown path. We may start out eager and confident, certain that we will reach our goals and our dreams. But as we travel, we can become confused about the direction we are going. The only way we can keep going is to keep our eye on the path before us.

Jesus leads us along the trails of our lives and guides us as we journey. Through scripture and prayer, we can travel through life with confidence. Christ will lead us and guide us and bring us safely to our journey's end.

Prayer: *Dear Jesus, help us to remain focused on your path. Give us courage to follow where you lead. Amen*

Thought for the day: I will follow Jesus each day.

Gilda Picioccio (New Jersey, US)

New hope

Read 1 Peter 5:6–10

Cast all your anxiety on [God] because he cares for you.
1 Peter 5:7 (NIV)

As the day for my annual colonoscopy approached, I was filled with anxiety that my cancer might have returned. Just one year earlier, the doctor had found and removed several non-cancerous polyps. Though I had 'beaten' colon cancer twice before, the 'what-ifs' overwhelmed me. Finally, I'd had enough. I was tired of feeling defeated.

I began to pray in a different way. I got really honest with God about how angry I was over my cancer diagnosis at the age of 17, and the high risk of cancers I face because of a rare genetic condition. I let myself grieve the loss of my health, my fertility, and my carefree teenage years. The tears flowed and flowed – until one day they stopped. I began to sense God's presence in my grief and started to notice how negative my thoughts had become. I resolved not to let negativity dominate me and instead focused on the positive things around me. They had been there all along, but I had needed God's help to see them.

When the day for my colonoscopy came, I looked for blessings. I found many: words of admiration for my strength, a warm blanket in the examination room, the blueberry muffin I ate on my way home, hugs from my family after the procedure, and a sense of freedom to share my story openly once again. Sometimes anxiety is inevitable, but when we recognise negative thoughts and let God show us the positives, our fears can be replaced by new hope.

Prayer: *Dear God, help us to trust you with our negative thoughts so that you can help us to see the blessings all around us. Amen*

Thought for the day: God helps me replace my anxieties with hope.

Danielle Ripley-Burgess (Missouri, US)

Darkness and light

Read Psalm 139:7–12

If I say, 'Surely the darkness shall cover me and the light about me be night,' even the darkness is not dark to you: the night is as bright as the day, for darkness is as light with you.

Psalm 139:11–12 (ESV)

I was returning from a cruise over the North Sea. At midnight there was still a primrose glow in the sky. Within a few hours it would be getting lighter, as the sun rose again. There was something deeply comforting in knowing that God was there, in the dimming light, in the short hours of darkness, and in the coming dawn. The sun is always there, whether it is below our horizon or visible to us. In the same way, God is always present, whether it feels to us as though we are in darkness or in light.

We cannot hide in the darkness or hide our darkness from God, 'for darkness is as light' to him. I have found this to be true in my own life. Things that have happened, or things I have done, that have caused me sadness, grief or shame, have been healed and transformed, over time, as I have brought them to Christ. He has promised 'I am the light of the world. Whoever follows me will not walk in darkness, but will have the light of life' (John 8:12, ESV).

Prayer: *Dear God, help me to bring you into any areas of darkness in my life, and let you fill them with your healing light and presence. Amen*

Thought for the day: We do not need to hide anything from God; his steadfast light shines on us all the time.

Gillian Tetmar (Somerset, England)

God, my shelter

Read Psalm 91:1–10

Whoever dwells in the shelter of the Most High will rest in the shadow of the Almighty.
Psalm 91:1 (NIV)

Some years ago, my brother-in-law Einar and I were hiking in the highlands of eastern Norway. We carried food, water and coffee as we walked along the tracks in an area between forest and mountain. At one point, the weather changed from sunshine to a heavy rainstorm. As the rain began, we hurried to find shelter under a large, twisted pine tree with a broad and dense canopy. We sat down under the tree, ate our lunch, drank our coffee and shared a wonderful time together.

Suddenly Einar said to me: 'Has it occurred to you that the psalmist might have experienced something like this when he wrote Psalm 91? I feel as if we are literally sheltered by our Lord at the moment.'

For a while, we sat without talking. And we felt the Lord embracing us. We did find shelter from the rainstorm that day, but more important is the everlasting promise of the Lord's shelter every day. It was as if the Lord had whispered to us, 'You can always rest in my shadow.'

Prayer: *Dear God, thank you for your everlasting love for us, and for your promise to hem us in and lay your hand upon us (see Psalm139:5). Amen*

Thought for the day: In the Lord's shade, I can find my shelter.

Øystein Brinch (Oslo, Norway)

Enough for all

Read Matthew 14:13–21

Jesus took the loaves, and when he had given thanks, he distributed them to those who were seated; so also the fish, as much as they wanted.
John 6:11 (NRSV)

It was my turn to help with the weekday lunch club at church, and it was evident that we were going to have a full house that day. A fellow volunteer looked out into the hall, counted 80 guests and announced that more people were on the way. The kitchen workers eyed each other nervously since the menu had been prepared with a modest crowd in mind. Slowly, we began to prepare the plates and serve them to the guests. When we finally looked up, we realised with amazement that every guest had been served. To our even greater surprise, we had enough food to offer second helpings.

When I think back on this event, I am reminded of Jesus feeding the multitudes. On that day in the kitchen we, like the disciples of Jesus, worried that we could not feed everyone. In the end, just as it was 2,000 years ago, God provided for our guests.

It is our human nature to worry that we might not have enough – enough food or time or money or talent. So we can become too afraid to give at all. But God is the great provider. When we are afraid, it is important to remember to put our trust in him and simply 'give them something to eat'.

Prayer: *O God, may we never tire of finding ways to feed those who are hungry. May all who hunger be filled. Amen*

Thought for the day: From my modest offerings God can create abundance.

Sherri Tuck (Virginia, US)

Humble hearts

Read Philippians 2:3–11
Humble yourselves therefore under the mighty hand of God, so that he may exalt you in due time.
1 Peter 5:6 (NRSV)

Years ago the minister at a retreat encouraged us to kneel in prayer to practise humility before God. This posture was new to me, but I knelt beside the other people there to bow before the Lord. I was so moved by that experience that I adopted a daily pattern of kneeling in prayer to show more reverence to God.

Now in my seventies and with arthritic knee pain, I can no longer kneel much. But I can still come before the Lord in humility because he sees beyond my physical posture to my heart. So whether I sit, stand or kneel, I can focus my worshipping heart on God.

God asks humility from all of us, but humility doesn't always come naturally. Sometimes it's difficult to admit we're wrong and ask for forgiveness, to serve others by doing menial tasks or refrain from boasting about our accomplishments. But Jesus is our ultimate example of humility. He became a man, served others and was obedient to death on a cross (see Philippians 2:8). So when we look to Jesus and ask God for help, we can grow in humility.

Prayer: *Dear Jesus, following your example, we ask that you help us to bow before God and worship in true humility. Amen*

Thought for the day: How shall I follow Jesus' example of humility?

Milton Harris (Washington, US)

The gift of prayer

Read James 5:13–16
The prayer of a righteous person is powerful and effective.
James 5:16 (NIV)

My husband had recently returned quite late from a church prayer meeting, and when I walked into the living room I expected to see him sitting in his comfortable recliner. But I was surprised to see him sitting on the sofa with his Bible open in front of him. I was used to seeing him reading his Bible and praying each morning, but not after a busy day and a long meeting.

I soon realised that his prayers weren't just quick 'bless this one and that one' prayers. Instead he searched God's word and used scripture verses to pray for each family member by name. Now, decades later, my husband's praying for our family remains the most beautiful sight at our home. Although he has a slight build and frail body, he is mighty in spirit and prayer. It comforts me to know that my husband daily intercedes for me and our children and grandchildren. What a priceless gift!

Prayer: *Heavenly Father, thank you for those who pray for us. Help us to follow Jesus' faithful example in praying for others. Amen*

Thought for the day: Prayer is a priceless gift that I can give.

Lydia Harris (Washington, US)

The elephant in the offertory plate

Read 2 Corinthians 9:10–15

Each of you must give as you have made up your mind, not reluctantly or under compulsion, for God loves a cheerful giver.
2 Corinthians 9:7 (NRSV)

The organist played and everyone finished singing the hymn. The stewards processed slowly to the front of the church, carrying the offertory plates. Everything was just as it should be except one thing. A small stuffed elephant sat on top of one of the offertory plates. The sight of the stuffed elephant combined with the serious faces of the stewards and the minister almost made me laugh out loud.

The minister prayed, offering the gifts to God, and the service continued. I sat thinking about that elephant and have thought about it since. What if it were the only thing that the giver had to give? It could have been something valuable to that person, a personal sacrifice.

Our gifts are not just our money but also our possessions and time, our talents and abilities, our love and care, our energy and passions. We are each unique in what we can offer to God. Who am I to laugh at an elephant in an offertory plate? Something I offer might surprise someone else. But it doesn't matter because the gifts are for God, who cares less about exactly what gifts we give than about our attitude as we give them.

Prayer: *Dear God, help us to be cheerful givers every day, pleasing you with our generosity and joy. Amen*

Thought for the day: All my gifts come from God, and I will share them with others.

Anne Miller (Ontario, Canada)

God is listening

Read 1 Chronicles 16:8–13

Seek the Lord and his strength, seek his presence continually.
1 Chronicles 16:11 (NRSV)

In my early days as a Christian, I struggled to understand the importance of prayer. I didn't see the point, and because of that my spiritual growth suffered.

Over time, I learned that without prayer I didn't really have a relationship with God. It was absurd to think that I could call him my friend without talking and spending time with him. So I went to some friends and people in my church and asked them questions such as, 'What are the right times to pray?' and 'What is the right way to pray?' I learned that praying is all about the heart. No matter what we say, God is always there.

Prayer is a journey into the great relationship we have with God. It is a privilege! Praying isn't about what we are doing; it's about what we are looking for – a deeper relationship with him. If we seek with open hearts, he will do the rest.

Prayer: *Dear God, help us to remember that we can pray to you anytime, anywhere, and about anything. Thank you for always listening. As Jesus taught us, we pray, 'Our Father in heaven, hallowed be your name, your kingdom come, your will be done, on earth as it is in heaven. Give us today our daily bread. Forgive us our debts, as we also have forgiven our debtors. And lead us not into temptation, but deliver us from the evil one.'* Amen*

Thought for the day: Praying to God is a wonderful privilege.

Thomas Warren (Texas, US)

*Matthew 6:9–13, NIV

Our foundation

Read Ephesians 2:19–22

No one can lay any foundation other than the one already laid, which is Jesus Christ.
1 Corinthians 3:11 (NIV)

During a hurricane several years ago, our home was flooded. After that experience, and because we live on a tidal creek, we decided to raise our house to prevent damage from any future storms. Once the house was lifted, we had to have a new foundation built. This took so long that we had to find another place to live for over two years while we waited for our house to be lifted and renovated.

During that stressful time, I became depressed and found it hard to get through each day. Then I started reading my study Bible and began to develop a deep and abiding relationship with Jesus. Not only did my house get a new foundation, but I began to build my life upon the solid foundation of Christ's teaching.

As believers, we are all a part of the same structure, the Church, and its chief cornerstone is Jesus Christ. The cornerstone of a foundation connects the walls and bears the weight of the building on itself – holding together the entire structure. That's what Jesus did when he died on the cross for us. He bore the weight of our sins, and now he connects us all by dwelling in us through the Holy Spirit. Our faith is built on Jesus Christ, and we can get through each day knowing that he and his love are the foundation for our lives.

Prayer: *Dear Lord, thank you for bearing the weight of our sins and lifting us up when we are in despair. Amen*

Thought for the day: I will make Jesus the cornerstone of my life.

Jan Towne (Virginia, US)

Preaching the gospel

Read 1 Thessalonians 2:9–13

The whole law is summed up in a single commandment, 'You shall love your neighbour as yourself.'
Galatians 5:14 (NRSV)

At one time during my childhood, my mum was my Sunday school teacher. She suggested we think of ourselves as a mirror, reflecting Christ's love to others through our actions.

For years, I kept hearing that it is necessary for Christians to witness for Christ. I assumed that this meant aggressively confronting non-Christians, and I was troubled.

I am less troubled, however, when I remember my mother's idea of reflecting Christ's love. It is still not in my nature to tell someone about Christ in a confrontational manner. Instead I find comfort in knowing that others can see God's love if I give Christ the credit for the love I express – whether face to face or in my devotional writing.

Sharing love is a way of preaching the gospel. Every one of us has the calling to share God's love with others. This work is our ultimate purpose in life. Sharing with others is serving others. We give to others what we receive from God. We are serving God by serving humanity, and our actions confirm our beliefs.

Prayer: *Thank you, God, for letting Christ shine through our lives to others. Help us to remember that it is your light that shines through us. Amen*

Thought for the day: How do I preach the gospel?

Dusty Reed (Nevada, US)

Made for the moment

Read Luke 12:22–28

Can any of you by worrying add a single hour to your span of life?
Luke 12:25 (NRSV)

I was feeling anxious. I wanted to know what my future held so that I could have control over it. But that was impossible. The more I thought about the future, the more worried and depressed I became. I decided to take a walk and ponder what I had for the moment. On my journey I was distracted by the sounds of the birds in the trees beside the road. The birds seemed happy and lively. I began to ask myself some basic questions that I had never considered. How do these birds save for their future? What do they possess that they can give to their coming children? Nothing! Those birds go through each day trying to survive without knowing what tomorrow will look like. They move at their own pace and time. They demonstrate that life is made for the moment.

This is why Christ told us that we should not worry about tomorrow, for tomorrow will take care of itself. Each moment we have is precious and can never be retrieved. If we follow Christ's teaching, we won't allow our worries to steal our joy because we will treasure this present moment and the next and the next.

Prayer: *Dear God, give us the courage to live in the moment and leave our worries to you. Amen*

Thought for the day: God's love remains constant through each and every moment.

Adedeji Adewunmi (Lagos, Nigeria)

Unfathomable grace

Read Ephesians 3:1–12

God gave his grace to me, the least of all God's people, to preach the good news about the immeasurable riches of Christ to the Gentiles.
Ephesians 3:8 (CEB)

There are more than 150 million objects in the Smithsonian Institution's collections. If a person were to go every day for eight hours and spend only two minutes on each item, it would take nearly 2,000 years to see them all. When I went, I looked at objects for much longer than two minutes. It would have taken me tens of thousands of years, and even then I wouldn't know the stories behind the objects.

Plumbing the depths of God offers infinitely more opportunity for mystery and discovery. Before Paul became a Christian, he lived his life as a strict, law-obeying Pharisee. When he began to understand God's plan for salvation through faith in Christ for both Jews and Gentiles, it must have been like entering the Smithsonian. Paul must have been dazzled by the overwhelming nature of this new discovery of grace. Every fresh insight revealed a new aspect of God's kindness and mercy. Paul often used words like unsearchable, incomprehensible and unfathomable to describe God's grace and love.

God invites us to explore these indescribable wonders, helping us declare with Paul, 'Oh, the depth of the riches of the wisdom and knowledge of God!' (Romans 11:33, NIV).

Prayer: *Dear God, give us eyes to see the unfathomable richness of your grace. Amen*

Thought for the day: The depth and breadth of God's love is dazzling!

Linda Barrett (Alabama, US)

A refuge for the wounded

Read Psalm 16:1–11

Let all who take refuge in you be glad; let them ever sing for joy.
Psalm 5:11 (NIV)

Several years ago I volunteered at a nature and science museum. My responsibilities included feeding and administering medication to the resident wildlife and cleaning their outdoor habitats. Several animals, including two bald eagles, had sustained injuries that hindered their survival in the wild. The birds were flightless because of bullet wounds to their wings. Whenever I entered their large, fenced enclosure, they'd lift their damaged, drooping wings and screech at me. Despite the wounds that altered their lives, the eagles survived because of the refuge of our museum.

In a spiritual sense, when wounds alter our lives, we too have a refuge. Whether we're suffering from physical injuries or struggling with emotional wounds like grief, God is our refuge. He heals us when we're hurting. After my brother's death, when wounds of loss altered my life, God turned my 'mourning into gladness' (Jeremiah 31:13) when I asked Jesus into my heart. And when my father died from cancer, God blessed a ministry that I started in his memory. I found myself 'sorrowful, yet always rejoicing' (2 Corinthians 6:10).

God can mend our broken hearts. In the refuge of his love we find solace that causes us to 'sing for joy'.

Prayer: *God of comfort and healing, thank you for being our refuge when we suffer from life's wounds. Amen*

Thought for the day: 'Blessed are all who take refuge in [the Lord]' (Psalm 2:12).

Debra Pierce (Massachusetts, US)

Real treasure

Read 1 Corinthians 1:4–9

The word of the Lord came to Abram in a vision: 'Do not be afraid, Abram. I am your shield, your very great reward.'
Genesis 15:1 (NIV)

An investment that would have provided me with a comfortable income did not work out. Consequently, I took a job that gave me a good income but also came with some challenging situations. Whenever the pressure at my job increased, I would feel regret and chagrin at the investment that could have saved me from this headache.

Recently, during worship, I poured out my heart in prayer, saying, 'Lord, why didn't it work out?' God didn't answer directly but did nudge me with the thought: 'Sarah, your greatest treasure is me. Your greatest asset is building a record of my faithfulness and goodness toward you.' Then I understood. Yes, it would have been 'easier' to provide for myself through the investment rather than through this job that put me in uncomfortable situations. But every day God's been helping me, giving me protection, comfort and wisdom – real help that I cannot deny. What I need most is to know that our good and faithful God is with me. Nothing is more valuable than knowing from experience that he is trustworthy.

Prayer: *Dear God, help us to trust that your faithfulness will last throughout eternity. Amen*

Thought for the day: Nothing is more valuable than God's love and faithfulness.

Sarah Eom (California, US)

A modern-day parable

Read Luke 10:25–37

Jesus told him, 'Go and do likewise.'
Luke 10:37 (NIV)

I was working at a construction site on a riverfront in Ahmadabad. My 'office' was made of sheets of metal from the site. Nearby a pool of water had formed as a result of the construction, and over time mud had collected.

One day a young cyclist fell into the muddy pool and lay there without moving. Residents from the nearby housing area gathered and decided among themselves that the young man surely must have been drunk – and they left him lying in the mud.

As I surveyed the situation, I looked at the cross hanging in my office, and a sense of compassion for the young man swept over me. As I bent down to him, I sensed no smell of alcohol; he had fallen because he was ill. From his identification papers, I found contact information for his family and called for an ambulance to take the young man to the hospital.

Later, as my family and I were discussing the event, we recalled that it had not been unlike Jesus' parable of the Good Samaritan. I was thankful for the cross hanging in my office and for God's strength to help me respond faithfully to Jesus' command to 'go and do likewise'.

Prayer: *Loving and merciful God, give us strength and encouragement always to help those in need. Amen*

Thought for the day: Whom is God calling me to help today?

Ramanbhai Rathod (Gujarat, India)

Distorted vision

Read Philippians 4:8–9

I press on toward the goal to win the prize for which God has called me heavenward in Christ Jesus.
Philippians 3:14 (NIV)

A black, spidery form appeared in my line of vision. I jumped as I swiped at it, but the black blob hovered. I splashed water in my eye and rubbed it, but the shadow remained and seemed to multiply. Later that evening, I thought I saw lightning strikes flashing in the corner of my eye.

Fearing a retinal tear or detachment, I contacted my optician. After examining my eye, she diagnosed me with a floater that obstructed the light coming into my eye, casting shadows on my retina. Thankfully, I had no damage to my retina. She instructed me not to focus my gaze on the floater but to look beyond the shadow. If I were to focus on the floater, the nerve impulses would be directed toward it, further distorting my vision. The brain is wired to strengthen what we focus on.

As I pondered this, I discovered a spiritual truth. If I focus my thoughts on murmuring and complaining about the negative things in my life, I will see only the negative. But if I choose to turn my gaze and focus on Jesus through prayer, praise and studying scripture, my vision will clear. I will be able to see beyond my circumstances to God's greatness and goodness.

Prayer: *Dear Lord, help us to focus on you and your will for us. Amen*

Thought for the day: Today, I will focus on the goodness of God.

Joanie Shawhan (Wisconsin, US)

Sunrise

Read Luke 1:67–79

[The Lord's] compassions never fail. They are new every morning; great is your faithfulness.
Lamentations 3:22–23 (NIV)

Early one autumn morning, I looked out of the window to see the house across the street backlit by the most amazing sunrise. The sky was a deep orange and soft peach. Dense pink clouds were streaked with vivid yellow, and blue appeared through the gaps in the clouds. This magnificent scene inspired gratitude and a sense of awe and wonder in me. It drew my focus to our Creator and to Christ, the light of the world who shines love on us each day.

The next day I awoke to yet another incredible sunrise. 'How faithful is our God!' I thought. Then the words from Lamentations came to mind, that the Lord's compassions never fail; they are new every morning. I marvelled that even in a book of passionate lament these words of hope declaring God's faithfulness would spring forth.

As the colours of the sunrise begin to fade, I can face each day with gladness and hope – joyful in the knowledge that we have a faithful God whose mercies are fresh every morning.

Prayer: *Thank you, Creator God, for daily reminders of the hope we have through your Son, Jesus Christ. Amen*

Thought for the day: I will look for signs of God's faithfulness today.

Julie Brown (Northern Ireland, UK)

PRAYER FOCUS: TO SEE GOD'S LOVE

Ordinary people

Read Mark 1:16–20
We have this treasure in jars of clay to show that this all-surpassing power is from God and not from us.
2 Corinthians 4:7 (NIV)

Jesus was walking beside the Sea of Galilee when he saw Simon and Andrew fishing. A little further down the lakeshore Jesus came upon James and his brother John. He called all four of them to join him. I have often wondered why Jesus chose these men to follow him. They weren't rich or famous; they were just ordinary fishermen. In fact they were probably some way down on the social ladder.

Jesus could have called anyone to be his followers. He could have selected leaders of commerce or learned priests from the synagogue. He could have selected high-ranking men from the Roman army or government officials. But no! Jesus selected four ordinary men to be the first of his closest associates – four ordinary men to carry on his ministry.

Jesus demonstrates vividly to all of us that he chooses ordinary people to follow him. Jesus requires no specific qualifications for those whom he calls. All he wants, as demonstrated in today's scripture reading, is for ordinary people to follow him. And in following, we discover who he truly is.

Prayer: *Open our ears and hearts, dear Christ, to hear your call to us each day. Amen*

Thought for the day: Jesus calls all people to follow him – no CV required.

Bob McCarthy (California, US)

Through the eyes of a child

Read Matthew 18:1–5

[Jesus] said, 'Truly I tell you, unless you change and become like little children, you will never enter the kingdom of heaven.'
Matthew 18:3 (NIV)

As my young son, André, and I waited at the doctor's waiting room, an elderly woman and her son came in and sat by us. Her son appeared to be around 50 years old and had some special needs. When the woman got up and left her son for just a few moments, he began to make involuntary sounds and movements. André kept looking at the man and asked me what was happening. A quick response at that moment would not have satisfied my son's curiosity. So I told him discreetly I would explain later. At that moment, the man extended his hand toward André to greet him and said, 'Hello.' André took his hand, greeted him, then turned to me and said, 'Mama, I know what it is.' 'Really?' I said hesitantly. 'Oh, yes. He has bit of a problem speaking, that's all.'

The words of Jesus in today's quoted scripture became very real for me that day in the actions of my young son. I was amazed that in that brief exchange, André didn't judge or focus on the things an adult might focus on. Instead of the man's disability, André saw his humanity. I believe Jesus calls us to do likewise.

Prayer: *God of hope, grant us the gift of understanding to see through the eyes of a child and learn to recognise the humanity in all your people. Amen*

Thought for the day: Children have much to teach me about God's kingdom.

Lilliam Hernández (Puerto Rico)

PRAYER FOCUS: PARENTS OF CHILDREN WITH SPECIAL NEEDS

Elisha's eyes

Read 2 Kings 6:8–17

'Oh no, my lord! What shall we do?' the servant asked… Elisha prayed, 'Open his eyes, Lord, so that he may see.'
2 Kings 6:15, 17 (NIV)

I can identify with Elisha's servant who stumbled out of bed to discover an army aligned against him. Like the servant, I have sometimes found myself surrounded by threatening circumstances – ominous medical diagnoses, financial strains, family crises. When normal life takes an adverse turn, it's easy to feel vulnerable and unprotected.

Like the frightened servant, we wonder what to do. I find hope in Elisha's reply. He allayed his servant's fear with a prayer! Elisha prayed for his servant to see what Elisha already saw – the protective presence of the Lord, shining in fiery array all around them. Yes, the threat of the enemy army was real, but God's protection was just as real. Elisha and his servant saw the reality of what the psalmist describes: 'As the mountains surround Jerusalem, so the Lord surrounds his people both now and for evermore' (Psalm 125:2). The landscape of our lives may change abruptly. Threatening circumstances may loom large. But we are always enfolded by the protective power of God.

Prayer: *Mighty Father, give us Elisha's eyes! Help us sense your watchful protection always surrounding us. Amen*

Thought for the day: I am always surrounded by God's protective power.

Marion Speicher Brown (Florida, US)

God is love

Read 1 John 4:7–12

Beloved, let us love one another, because love is from God.
1 John 4:7 (NRSV)

My dear high-school friend was bright, tender-hearted, and thought-ful; but she was not happy. One morning she did not come to school. I learned later that she had taken her own life. I was devastated. Many questions crossed my mind. What if I had talked to her more often about how she felt? Was there anything I could have done? How could I have missed the signs of trouble?

Many people at my school called my friend's suicide a sin. But from the Bible and from my church I had learned that God is love. It did not make sense to me that an all-loving God would condemn my friend because she could not bear the weight of life's harshness. I felt guilty, confused and fearful.

One of the reasons I chose Christian studies as my subject at college was to explore questions about God. I still do not have all the answers. Yet, I am passionate about proclaiming God's unconditional love and unlimited forgiveness. He loves us in our pains as well as joys, in life's valleys and on the mountains.

When I was at high school, I did not have the courage or certainty to assert that my friend was deeply loved by God. With confidence, I now proclaim that love is stronger than any condemnation, judgement or fear. God is love!

Prayer: *Loving God, may my words and actions reflect your great love today and always. Amen*

Thought for the day: God loves me in times of pain as well as in times of joy.

Hwa-Young Chong (Illinois, US)

PRAYER FOCUS: SOMEONE CONTEMPLATING SUICIDE

Spiritual fruit

Read Luke 6:43–49

Jesus said, 'Each tree is recognised by its own fruit.'
Luke 6:44 (NIV)

Before I set out on the path to ministry, church members were asked questions about me regarding my faith. Among the questions was this one: 'Does Ian show fruit?' I had never really understood what Jesus meant in the verse quoted above, but this question made me consider the analogy anew.

When I worked for a sales company, one of my colleagues was a man who was always smiling, laughing and pleasant to be around. Every one loved him for his spirit. One day while I was making a sales call, the person at the other end of the phone was rude to me. As I voiced my anger and frustration after the call, my colleague came into my office and said, 'I've had calls like that before. When I get them, I quickly pray to Jesus, smile, then make another call!' It was now clear to me why everyone was drawn to this man. He was bearing the fruit of a deep relationship with Christ, and many of us were hungry for this kind of spiritual strength.

Through my colleague's example I began to understand what Jesus meant by his words, 'Each tree is recognised by its own fruit', and to think about what this meant for my life as a minister. As life's challenges arise, others can see our fruit through the kindness and compassion we show them and by reflecting the peace of God within us.

Prayer: *Dear God, help us to take every opportunity to share with others the fruits of our relationship with you. Amen*

Thought for the day: What 'fruit' do I want others to see in me today?

Ian Bailey (North Carolina, US)

God is my strength

Read Philippians 4:10-13

I can do all things through Christ which strengtheneth me.
Philippians 4:13 (KJV)

I recently suffered from a bout of flu. I tried to accomplish my tasks as usual, but every time I tried, I felt dizzy. I prayed and asked God to heal me, but the illness only seemed to get worse. Eventually I started to feel better, and after about a week I was able to complete my tasks well, even though they all took a much longer time than usual.

All the time, I wondered why God did not heal me immediately so that I could finish everything I had to do on time. Then, while reading the Bible in my quiet time, I came upon today's quoted verse. It helped me to realise that although I was ill, God had given me strength to finish my tasks.

Sometimes the only way out of trouble is to push through it. When our prayers seem to go unanswered, we tend to worry and become afraid. But whatever happens in our lives, God is always with us. Our situations or circumstances may not always seem good, but we can persevere because we have a strong God.

Prayer: *Dear God, thank you for always being with us. Because of you, we are strong and can do all things. Amen*

Thought for the day: God gives me strength to do all that he has set before me.

Meliana Santoso (East Java, Indonesia)

In the crowd

Read Mark 5:25–34

Immediately aware that power had gone forth from him, Jesus turned about in the crowd and said, 'Who touched my clothes?'
Mark 5:30 (NRSV)

On a family holiday to New York City, I went to St Patrick's Cathedral thinking it would be a quiet place to pray and reflect during a break from our hectic pace of shopping and visiting museums. As I entered the cathedral, however, it seemed more like an exhibition hall than a place of worship. People walked around snapping photos. Some pointed out the arches and stained glass windows to companions. Small groups huddled in the alcoves, discussing statues and artefacts.

As I slipped into a pew, I wondered, 'Can I find God here with so much noise and activity?' Then I remembered the woman who fought her way through the crowd to touch the hem of Jesus' robe. Mark's Gospel tells us that people were pressing in on Jesus from all sides. Yet as healing power flowed out of him, Jesus turned and asked, 'Who touched my clothes?' The woman fell down before him, told her story, and was greeted by him as a daughter worthy of commendation.

The story helped me to see that the noise and distractions in the cathedral could not prevent my worship. Jesus knew I was there and would hear my prayer, even in the midst of the talkative sightseers. As Paul wrote, 'I'm convinced that nothing can separate us from God's love in Christ Jesus our Lord' (Romans 8:38, CEB).

Prayer: *Loving God, thank you for being with us in the crowded places as well as the quiet ones. Help us to remember that nothing can separate us from you. Amen*

Thought for the day: Nothing can prevent me from spending time with God.

Zoe Hicks (Georgia, US)

Small group questions

Wednesday 2 May

What do you think the phrase 'rooted in Christ' means? How do you see this in terms of your own faith?

How can we develop a strong foundation for our faith? What could you do each day to reinforce your foundation?

Think of someone you know who has helped you to develop your own faith. How would you describe them? In what ways has their faith helped you?

Have you ever been through a time when you felt that your faith was threatened? How did you feel? What helped you to keep hold of your faith during this time?

In what ways does your church community build up people's faith? Are there things that you can do to help this?

Wednesday 9 May

1 When you were a child, what were your parents adamant about? How did you feel about this practice?

2 Did you talk about faith with your friends when you were younger? If so, who initiated the conversations? Were those conversations difficult or easy? What can you remember about one or more of those conversations that made you uncomfortable?

3 What daily practices help you grow in your faith? Are these practices ones you developed on your own or that were taught to you by a parent or mentor?

4 Who are the spiritual leaders in your church? How do they model faith for others, especially those in younger generations? For whom are you a spiritual leader?

5 Which character from the Bible is your role model for faithful living? Why do you relate to this person particularly?

Wednesday 16 May

1 Think of a time when you experienced loss. How did that loss affect you? Who was with you during that time? How did that person support you?

2 What changes or new beginnings happened as a result of this loss? At the time, did those changes feel like gifts or burdens? Do you feel the same way about them now?

3 Some losses are expected, while others come as a shock. In your experience, are expected losses easier to navigate? Why or why not? What helps you prepare for expected losses or changes?

4 How does your church support and care for those who are experiencing loss or new beginnings? How could your church do this work better? How can you help?

5 What is God growing in your life at the moment? What excites you about how God is working with you? What worries you?

Wednesday 23 May

1 Have you ever had a powerful experience at a Christian retreat or event like the one today's writer describes? If so, describe your experience.

2 What verse or passage of scripture is most meaningful to you? Why that verse? How has it shaped your thinking and your actions?

3 When have you asked for forgiveness? From whom did you ask forgiveness? Was it difficult to ask? What happened?

4 How do the minister and leaders in your church talk about forgiveness? How do they model repentance and asking for forgiveness? How can you model forgiveness for others in your life?

5 Whom do you want to forgive? Have you prayed about this relationship? What do you need in order to move toward forgiving this person?

Wednesday 30 May

When have you felt the need to find your way back to God? What made you feel this way? How did you try to find God?

What practices help you to feel connected and close to God? What new practice would you like to try to help you strengthen your faith and your relationship with him?

3 When and where do you pray? How important is prayer to you? Is prayer part of your daily routine? How do you pray?

4 What are you most grateful for? How do you express your gratitude to God and to others?

5 Who among your friends and family most needs prayer today? What is your prayer for that person?

Wednesday 6 June

1 When have you been faced with a challenge for which you did not feel prepared? How did you overcome the challenge?

2 Describe a time in your life when God 'multiplied your efforts'. What did this experience teach you about God and what did it teach you about yourself?

3 Do you think God wants us to first try to do things on our own before asking for help? Why or why not?

4 Is it easy or difficult for you to ask for God's help? Why? Recall a time when you relied on your strength alone to accomplish a task. What difference might it have made in the situation had you asked God to intervene?

5 For what in your life would you ask God's help today?

Wednesday 13 June

1 Is any request too small or trivial to bring to God in prayer? Explain your answer.

2 When, where and from whom did you learn to pray? In what ways ha[s] your prayer life changed over time?

3 Do you think any of our prayers are ever a bother to God? Why or wh[y] not?

4 Recall some characters from scripture who prayed for small thing[s]. How did God answer their prayers? What do their stories teach u[s] about prayer?

5 Today's 'Thought for the day' says, 'God wants to hear all my con[cerns] – big and small.' Name one 'big' thing and one 'small' thin[g] about which you are praying this week.

Wednesday 20 June

1 When have you failed to see God's blessings because you wer[e] so focused on other things? How has this experience helped yo[u] become more aware of his blessings in your daily life?

2 Why do you think that it is sometimes easy to take God's blessing[s] for granted? What can you do to become more aware of the ways h[e] blesses you each day?

3 Sometimes people will say that something was a 'blessing in dis[-]guise'. What do you think they mean by the phrase 'blessing in dis[-]guise'? Have you ever received such a blessing?

4 Do you think God blesses some people more than others? Why woul[d] he heap blessings on some people while withholding blessings fro[m] others? Explain your answer.

5 Name some of the blessings for which you are thankful to God today[.] In the coming week, how will you be more attentive to the blessing[s] he has given you?

Wednesday 27 June

1 Have you ever had an experience similar to the writer of today's med[-]itation in which you were reluctant to serve but you were glad yo[u] did? What did you learn from this experience?

2 With what attitude does God want us to serve others? Support your answer with scripture.

3 Is it ever possible to become overextended in our commitments to serve others? What are some ways we can care for others while also caring for ourselves?

4 Choose a story from one of the four Gospels in which Jesus serves a person or group of people. What attributes of Jesus' service in this story would you like to emulate in your own service to others?

5 What opportunities to serve God by serving others does your church community offer? What opportunities would you like it to offer? In what three specific ways will you go above and beyond in serving God this week?

Wednesday 4 July

1 Acts 20:35 says, 'It is more blessed to give than to receive' (NRSV). Relate an experience when this was true for you.

2 Were you to switch places with the writer of today's meditation, how would you have responded to the farmer's offer? Would you have taken him up on it? Why or why not? Why do you think many people did not?

3 When has someone done a favour for you that was both unexpected and meaningful? What is most memorable about this favour? How has it made you a better neighbour to others?

4 When was the last time you gave generously without expecting anything in return? Are there times when we should expect something in return?

5 What do you think would happen if we showed generosity to another person each time someone showed generosity to us? What difference would it make in our communities?

Wednesday 11 July

1   If you were to make a list of ten things that you are thankful for today, what would your list include?

2   Have you ever been in a situation where it was hard to sense God's faithfulness? How would you encourage someone going through a similar experience? What would you do differently were you to be in a situation like that again?

3   Name some passages of scripture that illustrate God's faithfulness to us. Which of these is your favourite? What parallels do you see between the ways God helped the people in scripture and the ways he helps you in your life today?

4   When on your walk of faith have you struggled with doubt? What helped you overcome your doubt? Is it OK to have times in our lives when we doubt God's faithfulness?

5   Do you have an object that helps remind you of God's faithfulness – a meaningful note written by a friend, a Bible given to you on a special occasion, a photograph? Why is this object a good reminder to you of God's faithfulness?

Wednesday 18 July

1   Do you feel that you can speak honestly with God about your fears? What would help you to be more honest with him?

2   The 'Thought for the day' says, 'God already knows my weaknesses – and loves me anyway.' Tell a story from your life about a time when you felt clearly how much God loved you despite your weaknesses.

3   Have you ever felt abandoned by God? Do you think this is something that all Christians experience at some point? What should we do when we feel that God has abandoned us?

4   The writer of today's meditation says, 'I can be honest with God even when my emotions aren't positive or reverent.' Do you agree or disagree with this statement? Use scripture to support your answer.

5 When has God worked through you to accomplish something, even though you did not feel up to the task? What did you learn from this experience?

Wednesday 25 July

1 When have you prayed for something specific only to have God give you something different? How did you feel about this at the time? How do you feel about it now? Why do you think God sometimes gives us something other than what we ask for?

2 Talk about a time when God used you to serve others in an unexpected way. How did this help you to understand the differences between your plans and priorities and the plans that God has for you? Was it easy or difficult for you to follow God's plans over your own?

3 How should we respond to God when he leads us in a direction that we do not want to go or intend to go? Have you ever resisted God's leading? Does he ever lead us in the wrong direction?

4 When have you been confused about the direction in which God was leading you? What gave you clarity? How can we be certain that we are doing what he wants us to do?

5 What do you do for a living? Do you enjoy your job? In what ways do you serve God at your place of employment? In what ways could you serve him better?

Wednesday 1 August

1 What does it mean to you to focus your thoughts on God? Name some specific practices that help you to do this.

2 The writer of today's meditation says, 'Studying God's word shapes our minds and changes the way we think.' Do you agree or disagree? Give an example from your own life to support your answer.

3 Do you think memorising scripture is important? Why or why not? What value might there be in memorising scripture?

4 How often do you read and study the Bible? Have you ever read the Bible in its entirety from cover to cover? What was this experience like for you? Did you learn anything that you might not have learned otherwise? Is it important that Christians read the entire Bible? Do you think it is possible to know everything about the Bible?

5 When have you read something in scripture that was surprising or startling? Has it ever been frustrating? How did this change the way you read and understand scripture? How did it change your understanding of God?

Wednesday 8 August

1 Talk about a time when you felt overwhelmed by the 'what-ifs'. Where and to whom did you turn for strength and encouragement? What words of hope would you offer to someone overwhelmed by the 'what-ifs' today?

2 When were you last so consumed by negative thoughts that you could not see all that was positive around you? What helps you focus more on the positive?

3 Today's meditation says, 'Sometimes anxiety is inevitable.' Do you agree or disagree with this statement? Why?

4 Why is it sometimes so easy to let fear and worry overtake us? Name some things that help you deal with fear and worry in your life. Is it ever possible to eliminate fear and worry from our lives?

5 1 Peter 5:7 says, 'Cast all your anxiety on [God] because he cares for you' (NIV). What does it mean to cast our anxiety on God? Name some spiritual practices that can help us do this. What is to be gained by giving our worries to him?

Wednesday 15 August

1 How important is prayer to you? How often do you think God wants us to pray? How is praying to him a privilege?

2 Do you think God has any expectations about how we pray and what we say? If so, what are they? Support your answer with scripture. In addition to prayer, in what other ways can we spend time with God?

3 How has your prayer life changed over time? What has caused it to change? How do you think it will continue to change?

4 The writer of today's meditation asks two questions: 'What are the right times to pray?' and 'What is the right way to pray?' How would you answer these questions?

5 What concerns in your Christian community will you pray about in the week ahead? What will you ask God for in your prayers this week? For what will you give him thanks?

Wednesday 22 August

1 Have you ever witnessed a 'modern-day parable' such as the one described in today's meditation? Describe the experience.

2 What is your favourite parable? Why is it your favourite? What is most significant to you about it? In what ways has it influenced you as a Christian? When has one of Jesus' parables guided the way you responded to a situation?

3 Which of Jesus' parables challenges you the most? How does it challenge you? What do you not understand about it? What do you admire about it?

4 Why do you think Jesus so often spoke in parables? What value is there in telling a parable compared to conveying information in other ways? If you could ask Jesus one question about any one of his parables, what would it be?

5 When was the last time you helped someone in need? Can you recall a time when you were reluctant to help someone? Why were you reluctant? Is there ever a time when we should not help someone?

Wednesday 29 August

1 Who has inspired and encouraged you as a Christian? In what ways did this person inspire and encourage you? For whom in your life would you like to do the same?

2 The 'Thought for the day' asks, 'What "fruit" do I want others to see in me today?' How would you answer this question?

3 Were you to choose one scripture verse to live out in your life each day, what would the verse be and why? What about this would challenge you? What would make it rewarding?

4 The writer's colleague gave him some simple and practical ways to get through the situation. What are some simple and practical ways that help you to deal with similar situations? What difference does being a Christian make in how we approach scenarios that frustrate us and make us angry?

5 Galatians 5:22–23 refers to the fruit of the Spirit: 'love, joy, peace, forbearance, kindness, goodness, faithfulness, gentleness and self-control' (NIV). Is one of these more important than the others? Why or why not? Which of these would you like to practise more fully in your life?

Journal page

Journal page

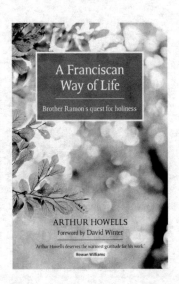

Brother Ramon was a much-loved writer and speaker who died in 2000 – a man who delighted in life and people, and who chose solitude to practise the presence of God. This first biography, written by his friend, has warmth and spiritual insight. It tells of his life's pilgrimage, his quest for holiness as a Franciscan friar, his love of God and his influence on others. The selection from his writings which concludes the book illustrates his spiritual journey, his views on ecumenism, contemplative prayer, spirituality, retreats, solitude, quietness and much more. It will be an inspiration to readers to live lives fully for Jesus Christ.

A Franciscan Way of Life
Brother Ramon's quest for holiness
Arthur Howells, with a foreword by David Winter
978 0 85746 662 4   £8.99
brfonline.org.uk

Anxious Times

Carmel Thomason

Foreword by Archbishop John Sentamu

A book of 24 undated reflections drawing on a range of relevant Bible passages to offer genuine hope and encouragement in anxious times. Encompassing the very human emotions of fear and anxiety, the reflections encourage us to draw comfort and strength from God's word even in those times when he seems silent to us. This book acknowledges that trust and hope in God's goodness doesn't always come easily, but when embraced we gain the strength to face our fear with courage and confidence.

Anxious Times

Carmel Thomason, with a foreword by Archbishop John Sentamu

978 0 85746 660 0 £3.99

brfonline.org.uk

Where do we turn when our world is falling apart? It takes courage to hope: to stand in our confusion and grief and still to believe that 'God is not helpless among the ruins'. Guided by Habakkuk and his prophetic landmarks, this book is a reflective journey through the tangled landscape of bewildered faith, through places of wrestling and waiting, and on into the growth space of deepened trust and transformation. Read it and learn the value and practice of honest prayer, of surrender, of silence and listening, and of irresistible hoping.

God among the Ruins
Trust and transformation in difficult times
Mags Duggan, with a foreword by Tony Horsfall
978 0 85746 575 7 £7.99
brfonline.org.uk

If faith is 'being sure of what we hope for and certain of what we do not see', what does that look like in practice today? In a world that is largely unsure and uncertain, how do we gain our confidence? *Faith in the Making* recognises the problem and seeks the answer in the list of faithful heroes found in Hebrews 11. This accessible, devotional resource will inspire individuals and groups to live more confidently for God in today's world. Heroic faith is far more attainable than we often think!

Faith in the Making
Praying it, talking it and living it
Lyndall Bywater, with a foreword by Danielle Strickland
978 0 85746 555 9 £7.99
brfonline.org.uk

How to encourage Bible reading in your church

BRF has been helping individuals connect with the Bible for over 90 years. We want to support churches as they seek to encourage church members into regular Bible reading.

Order a Bible reading resources pack

This pack is designed to give your church the tools to publicise our Bible reading notes. It includes:

- Sample Bible reading notes for your congregation to try.
- Publicity resources, including a poster.
- A church magazine feature about Bible reading notes.

The pack is free, but we welcome a £5 donation to cover the cost of postage. If you require a pack to be sent outside the UK or require a specific number of sample Bible reading notes, please contact us for postage costs. More information about what the current pack contains is available on our website.

How to order and find out more

- Visit **biblereadingnotes.org.uk/for-churches**.
- Telephone BRF on +44 (0)1865 319700 Mon–Fri 9.15–17.30.
- Write to us at BRF, 15 The Chambers, Vineyard, Abingdon OX14 3FE.

Keep informed about our latest initiatives

We are continuing to develop resources to help churches encourage people into regular Bible reading, wherever they are on their journey. Join our email list at **biblereadingnotes.org.uk/helpingchurches** to stay informed about the latest initiatives that your church could benefit from.

Introduce a friend to our notes

We can send information about our notes and current prices for you to pass on. Please contact us.

Subscriptions

The Upper Room is published in January, May and September.

Individual subscriptions
The subscription rate for orders for 4 or fewer copies includes postage and packing:
The Upper Room annual individual subscription   £16.95

Group subscriptions
Orders for 5 copies or more, sent to ONE address, are post free:
The Upper Room annual group subscription   £13.50

Please do not send payment with order for a group subscription. We will send an invoice with your first order.

Please note that the annual billing period for group subscriptions runs from 1 May to 30 April.

Copies of the notes may also be obtained from Christian bookshops.

Single copies of *The Upper Room* cost £4.50.

Prices valid until 30 April 2019.

Giant print version
The Upper Room is available in giant print for the visually impaired, from:

Torch Trust for the Blind
Torch House
Torch Way
Northampton Road
Market Harborough   Tel: +44 (0)1858 438260
LE16 9HL   torchtrust.org

THE UPPER ROOM: INDIVIDUAL/GIFT SUBSCRIPTION FORM

**All our Bible reading notes can be ordered online by visiting
biblereadingnotes.org.uk/subscriptions**

❏ I would like to take out a subscription myself (complete your name and address details once)
❏ I would like to give a gift subscription (please provide both names and addresses)

Title .... First name/initials .... Surname ....

Address ....

.... Postcode ....

Telephone .... Email ....

Gift subscription name ....

Gift subscription address ....

.... Postcode ....

Gift message (20 words max. or include your own gift card):

....

....

Please send *The Upper Room* beginning with the September 2018 / January 2019 / May 2019
issue (delete as appropriate):

Annual individual subscription ❏ £16.95   Total enclosed £ ....

Method of payment

❏ Cheque (made payable to BRF) ❏ MasterCard / Visa

Card no. ⬚⬚⬚⬚ ⬚⬚⬚⬚ ⬚⬚⬚⬚ ⬚⬚⬚⬚

Valid from ⬚⬚⬚⬚   Expires ⬚⬚⬚⬚

Security code* ⬚⬚⬚   *Last 3 digits on the reverse of the card
ESSENTIAL IN ORDER TO PROCESS THE PAYMENT

THE UPPER ROOM GROUP SUBSCRIPTION FORM

**All our Bible reading notes can be ordered online by visiting
biblereadingnotes.org.uk/subscriptions**

❑ Please send me .... copies of **The Upper Room** September 2018 / January 2019 /
May 2019 issue (*delete as appropriate*)

Title .... First name/initials .... Surname ....

Address ....

.... Postcode ....

Telephone .... Email ....

Please do not send payment with this order. We will send an invoice with your first order.

Christian bookshops: All good Christian bookshops stock BRF publications. For your
nearest stockist, please contact BRF.

Telephone: The BRF office is open Mon–Fri 9.15–17.30. To place your order, telephone
+44 (0)1865 319700.

Online: brf.org.uk

❑ Please send me a Bible reading resources pack to encourage Bible reading in
my church

Please return this form with the appropriate payment to:
BRF, 15 The Chambers, Vineyard, Abingdon OX14 3FE

To read our terms and find out about cancelling your order, please visit **brfonline.org.uk/terms**.

The Bible Reading Fellowship is a Registered Charity (233280)

UR0218

ɔ order

line: **brfonline.org.uk**
ephone: +44 (0)1865 319700
ɔn–Fri 9.15–17.30

Delivery times within the UK are normally 15 working days. Prices are correct at the time of going to press but may change without prior notice.

itle	Price	Qty	Total
Franciscan Way of Life	8.99		
nxious Times	3.99		
od among the Ruins	7.99		
aith in the Making	7.99		

POSTAGE AND PACKING CHARGES			
Order value	UK	Europe	Rest of world
Under £7.00	£2.00	£5.00	£7.00
£7.00–£29.99	£3.00	£9.00	£15.00
£30.00 and over	FREE	£9.00 + 15% of order value	£15.00 + 20% of order value

Total value of books	
Postage and packing	
Donation	
Total for this order	

ease complete in **BLOCK CAPITALS**

Title .... First name/initials .... Surname ....

Address ....

.... Postcode ....

Acc. No. .... Telephone ....

Email ....

Method of payment

☐ Cheque (made payable to BRF)   ☐ MasterCard / Visa

Card no. ☐☐☐☐ ☐☐☐☐ ☐☐☐☐ ☐☐☐☐ ☐☐☐☐

Valid from M M Y Y   Expires M M Y Y   Security code* ☐☐☐
Last 3 digits on the reverse of the card

Signature* .... Date .... / .... / ....
*ESSENTIAL IN ORDER TO PROCESS YOUR ORDER

The Bible Reading Fellowship Gift Aid Declaration

giftaid it

Please treat as Gift Aid donations all qualifying gifts of money made
☐ today, ☐ in the past four years, ☐ and in the future **or** ☐ My donation does not qualify for Gift Aid.
I am a UK taxpayer and understand that if I pay less Income Tax and/or Capital Gains Tax in the current tax year than the amount of Gift Aid claimed on all my donations, it is my responsibility to pay any difference.
Please notify BRF if you want to cancel this declaration, change your name or home address, or no longer pay sufficient tax on your income and/or capital gains.

lease return this form to: BRF, 15 The Chambers, Vineyard, Abingdon OX14 3FE | **enquiries@brf.org.uk**
ˉo read our terms and find out about cancelling your order, please visit **brfonline.org.uk/terms**.

The Bible Reading Fellowship (BRF) is a Registered Charity (233280)

Transforming
lives and communities

Christian growth and understanding of the Bible

Resourcing individuals, groups and leaders in churches for their own
spiritual journey and for their ministry

Church outreach in the local community

Offering three programmes that churches are embracing
to great effect as they seek to engage
with their local communities
and transform lives

Teaching Christianity in primary schools

Working with children and teachers to explore Christianity creatively
and confidently

Children's and family ministry

Working with churches and families to explore Christianity creatively
and bring the Bible alive

Visit **brf.org.uk** for more information on BRF's work

brf.org.uk

The Bible Reading Fellowship (BRF) is a Registered Charity (No. 233280)